Essex Works.
For a better quality of life

ONG

R. 4/1/12

Please return this book on or before the date shown above. To renew go to www.essex.gov.uk/libraries, ring 0845 603 7628 or go to any Essex library.

Essex County Council

EXPLORING HISTORICAL ESSEX

ROBERT LEADER

The
History
Press

First published 2010

The History Press
The Mill, Brimscombe Port
Stroud, Gloucestershire, GL5 2QG
www.thehistorypress.co.uk

British Library Cataloguing in Publication Data.
A catalogue record for this book is available from the British Library.

ISBN 978 0 7524 5764 2

Typesetting and origination by The History Press
Printed in Great Britain
Manufacturing managed by Jellyfish Print Solutions Ltd

Contents

INTRODUCTION

The prime glory of Essex has to be its marvellous maritime heritage. Between the Stour and the Thames there are a multitude of waterways, river mouths and estuaries, creeks and marshes. They are the haunts of sailors and fishermen, and once the havens of old time smugglers.

Inland too, Essex has a rewarding diversity of endless attractions, flower-draped cottages, thatched villages, mediaeval market towns, castles and abbeys; the cool splendours of Epping Forest, and a windmill or a church tower peeping over almost every wooded hilltop.

It is all within easy reach of London, growing ever more rural and idyllic as the ripples of fields and woodlands spread northward from the M25. The county is a joy to explore, following the wanderings of the river valleys from their sources to the sea. The rivers were always the main corridors of exploration, colonisation and trade, and the villages and towns that have grown up along their banks all have a story to tell. From the Charm of the Chelmer to the Blackwater by-ways, every twist and turn finds a new delight. Essex is a county to savour at leisure.

Robert Leader, 2010

CHAPTER ONE

SWEET THAMES FLOW SOFTLY

The Thames has always been a river of dreams, exemplified in the line 'Sweet Thames flow softly', from the popular nostalgic folk song by The Spinners. In centuries past, sailors and explorers, merchants and adventurers, have all journeyed down the river from London to seek their fortunes and destiny, while others from afar have sailed up the river on a similar quest or enterprise. For all of them the low Essex shore was always their first and last glimpse of England.

Up until the middle of the last century, British ships sailing out of the Port of London dominated the trade routes of the world. The Cunard Queens ruled the Atlantic. Royal Mail Lines carried passengers to Brazil and South America, with some of their ships pushing up the Amazon as far as Iquitos.; P&O and Orient lines serviced Hong Kong, Japan and Australia.; the New Zealand Shipping Line sailed to Australia and New Zealand; and the liners of Union Castle circumnavigated Africa. All those once familiar names have disappeared now, and modern container ships and plush cruise ships have replaced almost all of the old passenger-cargo lines that once flew the Red Duster into every ocean of the world.

Times have changed, but there are is an endless variety of ships using the Thames, and as you begin to pass the Essex shore the river is now overshadowed by the magnificent Queen Elizabeth II Dartford Suspension Bridge, which was opened in 1991. Cars flow continuously overhead on the congested arc of the M25, and four concrete towers with their spider-web tracery of cables soar into the sky.

However, the rest of the long, flat Essex shoreline, which many a young sailor used to watch with either the slight tang of immediate homesickness, or the buoyant elation of homecoming, is still pretty much unchanged. Most sailors had their minds fixed on more exotic places at the far end of each voyage, but they were missing something, for there is much to be explored and enjoyed along the Essex side of the great river.

Cruise ships still come up to Tilbury, where the old passenger liners used to pick up and disembark passengers before making the last lap up to KG5 or Victoria docks, but

Tilbury has expanded and is now the principal container port for the Port of London. It is also the site of the huge, star-shaped, moated and earth-walled fort that is the best preserved of all the fortifications that were once strung out along both river banks to guard London's most vulnerable gateway.

There was a blockhouse here at the time of the Spanish Armada, and the present Tilbury Fort was built to replace it in the late seventeenth century. It was regularly garrisoned through the Napoleonic wars and through the First World War. There has always been the possible threat of an enemy fleet – our mercantile rivals the Spanish, the Dutch, the French, and finally the Germans.

The big artillery pieces still point out from the east and west gun lines along the embankment and it is still possible to see a Royal Navy destroyer and an old, red-sailed Thames sailing barge moving together up the river. The navy ship gleaming grey and sleek in the sunshine, brisk and direct about her business, while the barge tacks slowly and lazily, a poignant image of a bygone age.

Follow the river and you will come to Canvey Island, which is connected to the mainland by the bridge at South Benfleet. The island was once a lonely wasteland of mudflats and tidal inlets, until the land was reclaimed and protected by a series of embankments and drainage dykes built by a Dutch engineer in 1623. Despite this, the island is still vulnerable to exceptional tidal flooding. In 1953 the terrible combination of North Sea storms and spring tide surge that devastated the whole of the eastern county's coastlines, swamped Canvey and drowned fifty-eight people. However, that

The Thames has seen it all. Here a modern warship and an old Thames sailing barge sail under the guns and ramparts of Tilbury Fort.

hasn't stopped it from filling up with summer cottages and camper sites. Small pleasure craft abound, as it is especially popular with the boating fraternity.

Canvey is now also the site of a huge petroleum refinery, a gigantic mass of storage tanks and writhing pipelines, like the silver steel entrails of some distorted industrial monster laid bare.

One of the best views of the whole island is from the ruins of Hadleigh Castle, which overlook the vast sweep of the estuary. Hadleigh Castle was built in the eleventh century to guard the mouth of the Thames, and for centuries its great stone towers and walls stood equal to the task. Sadly, today only the south-east tower remains intact, with a few crumbling walls marking the rest of the site, and the split wall of the north-east tower standing like some great shattered tooth.

A few miles further down the river is Old Leigh, once a small fishing community overlooking a small marshy inlet; the village has now been virtually swallowed up by the expansion of sprawling Southend. However, the flavour of Old Leigh is still there, with its cobbled High Street, rows of fishermen's cottages and a handful of fishing boats moored up among the pleasure craft at its old wharves.

There is an old black clapboard sail maker's loft at Victoria Wharf. A small pleasure yacht was moored at the quay and nearby was a small sandy beach where families played and sunbathed.

Not far away was the Essex Yacht Club, where scores of young people were bobbing around in bright-sailed small boats, or wrestling with them up and down the slipways

The ruins of Hadleigh Castle still overlook the Thames.

A few fishing boats still work from the harbour at Old Leigh.

on either side of the ex-navy minesweeper *Wilton,* which now serves as the clubhouse. It has replaced the *Bembridge,* the old pilot cutter that was the clubhouse from 1976 to 2004. Club racing events are monitored from the bridge and there are fine sea views over the bows.

During the Georgian period, the south end of Prittlewell became a small, fashionable seaside resort for the well-to-do. It was a place of sedate beach huts from where ladies in knee and elbow length bathing suits discreetly emerged to paddle in the sea. From there it expanded rapidly.

With the coming of the railway in 1856, Southend was only an hour away from the capital and promptly became the favourite holiday resort for the east end of London. The town is practically divided by the protruding pier, with the amusement arcades, fast rides and the children's paradise of Adventure Island lying on either side. To the left of the pier is the wild, brash and noisy face of Southend, the centre of all the bright lights, fish and chip shops and fun. Go to the right and you will find the more genteel aspects, with all the peace and beauty of its many manicured lawns and cliff top flower gardens.

Go up from the promenade and walk along the Royal Terrace, where the Royal Hotel was built in 1791 to commemorate a visit by Princess Caroline, the wife of the then Prince of Wales. Her visit helped to further establish the fashionable reputation of Southend. The terrace was restored in 1978, and in summer there is usually a vast array of glorious, multi-coloured hanging baskets decorating the modern hotel fronts.

Above: Massed flower baskets make a
glorious display along the Royal Terrace.

Right: On sunny afternoons the Victorian
bandstand is still the place for good
old-fashioned music and dancing.

Further along the white statue of Queen Victoria, flanked by palm trees, overlooks rich red and yellow rose beds; beside her there used to be an elegant Victorian bandstand where waltzing couples would glide gracefully on sunny afternoons. A cliff fall made it unsafe, so the bandstand has now been moved and re-opened in Priory Park.

In Priory Park stands the old Prittlewell Priory which was once a Cluniac monastery and is now a museum. Beside it stands the solid grey Crow Stone, which once stood on the beach at Chalkwell to mark the eastern extent of London's jurisdiction.

Prittlewell Square is Southend's oldest surviving park. It has a central high-splashing fountain, framed in the white wrought-iron entrance gates. Everywhere in Southend there are sumptuous flower beds and in summer the town is a rich chequerboard of green lawns and vibrant colours.

Down on the western esplanade is where the annual London to Southend Classic Car Rally finishes, usually with 300 or more vintage vehicles assembled there on the big day. This is just one of the annual events in this pleasure-geared seaside resort, ranging from the Old Leigh Regatta and the Thames Sailing Barge Match, both held out on the river, to the high-flying air show in the skies above.

If you can't face an hour's brisk walk, a full size train now takes you out to the far end of the pier, which for the passing sailor was either the last glimpse or first sight of the mouth of the Thames. The pier was built in 1889 and has survived seven boat crashes and four fires. The last blaze in October 2005 destroyed the old pier head railway station, but the trains still run and a multi-million pound reconstruction of the pier head is under way. One and a third miles long, it is the longest pier in the world.

Rows of fishermen cast their lines over the rails, hoping to haul a fat bass or mullet up on to the deck boards, and there is a pier head viewing tower with wide-ranging views. From here anything from a cockle boat to an oil tanker may hove into view.

Shoeburyness occupies the last elbow of land before the shoreline turns away to the north. Until the middle of the eighteenth century it was a smuggler's haven of misty marshes and hidden creeks; but with the founding of the Royal Artillery Garrison and School of Gunnery, the village began to grow. Between the wars its safe bathing beaches made it a holiday destination.

Plans have been put forward for another barrier here to span the full mouth of the Thames. London and the marshlands of Essex have always been vulnerable to flooding, due to the slow increase of river and sea levels over the centuries, and now that rate of increase is accelerating due to global warming. The Thames Barrier up the river at Greenwich, which was officially opened in 1984, is no longer considered adequate protection for the nation's capital. Flood and storm tides of the 1953 variety are predicted as a high probability, so the ongoing battle against the hungry sea will continue. If the proposed barrier is built it will be a massive structure stretching far into the marshes on either side, which will change the shore and skyline for ever.

The train takes the strain on the mile long ride to the end of Southend Pier.

However, for the moment the Thames has reached the cold North Sea without further hindrance. Having started far inland in the Cotswolds, passing through the great heart of London, and caressing the winding Essex shore, the river still flows by in all its many moods, timeless and continuous, on its romantic way to the far, wide world.

CHAPTER TWO

FOLLOWING THE STOUR

For the first twenty miles or so of its long meandering course, the Stour flows southward down through Suffolk and then turns east towards the sea to become the northern county border with Essex. The well-known towns of Clare, Sudbury and Nayland, all lie mainly on the Suffolk bank, but where the river reaches tranquil Dedham Vale, the heart of Constable Country, the claim to one of England's best loved tourist areas is shared equally with Essex.

Dedham itself lies on the Essex side, a charming little village which prospered with the cloth trade in the Middle Ages. The delightful High Street is full of buildings with Tudor interiors and Georgian façades. Although John Constable lived at East Bergholt in Suffolk, he was educated at the old Georgian grammar school here in Dedham. He would have crossed the Stour twice a day, going to and from school. Churches were among his favourite subjects, and the solid, square-tower Church of St Mary, built in the fifteenth century by a local cloth manufacture, features in several of his works.

Merrily down the river – boating on the Stour.

Dedham, where John Constable went to school.

Constable found the inspiration for his marvellous light-rich paintings in both counties, exploring and capturing on canvas every aspect of the fields and countryside that took his fancy. 'I associate my careless boyhood with all that lies on the banks of the Stour,' he wrote to a friend in 1821. 'Those scenes made me a painter and I am grateful.' We should be grateful too, not only for the wonderful paintings he left behind, but for drawing our attention to the lasting charm and beauty of one of the most delightfully pastoral corners of England. At Flatford, the classic view of Willy Lott's Cottage where he painted the *Hay Wain* is found on the Suffolk side, but the equally famous view of the mill pool can only be seen from Essex. Constable's father owned the mill there, and at first young John was destined to become a miller, learning the trade in his father's three mills. So this was one of his favourite haunts, and the source of some of his best loved paintings.

The lovely old, wooden bridge at Flatford spans both counties. It is a humped rustic arch, in the summertime it usually groans with the weight of visitors watching the waterborne antics of those in the boats below. There are rowing boats for hire both here and at Dedham, so this part of the river, flanked by old willows under the idle gaze of sleepy cows and strolling walkers, can be full of amateur sailors gliding lazily by. The Stour Valley path runs for sixty miles along the river's length, but this short stretch along the Essex bank must be the most popular walk of all.

The old wooden bridge
linking Suffolk and Essex
across the Stour.

The river continues seaward and within a few miles leaves its sheltered banks of fields and willows and opens out into the wider estuary where we find the two small ports of Manningtree and Mistley. This is where, in pre-Victorian times, the old horse-drawn Stour lighters would transfer their cargoes into larger, sail-driven barges for their continuing journey into the wider world. Grain, flour, malt and wool went outward to London. Coal came inward from Newcastle and timber from the Baltic; these would then be offloaded into the lighters to be hauled upriver to Sudbury. All has changed now. Where there were once the heaving masts and sturdy brown sails of commercial shipping, there are now only a few working fishing boats among what are mainly pleasure boats, moored or passing between the wide low-tide mudflats. The views across the Stour estuary are changed for ever. Manningtree was established as a town and port in the thirteenth century, and Mistley in the eighteenth century. Both ports were important brewing centres and both thrived in Georgian times. Many of their finest buildings date from that period. Manningtree has the dubious distinction in that it was here that Matthew Hopkins, Cromwell's awful Witch-finder General, began his fanatical career. He condemned a coven of supposed witches and watched them hanged on the village green. He was paid 20*s* for each witch discovered, terrorised the whole of England, and in the space of a year managed to hang sixty women in Essex alone. Hopkins was eventually exposed as a fraud and was himself hanged as a sorcerer. His body is buried on Mistley Heath. The road from Manningtree to Mistley follows the Stour and the estuary walls. The salt marsh and mudflats along the river are now a food-rich nature reserve for waders and wildfowl. Halfway between the two towns a large colony of swans congregate by a viewing point and information board, waiting to be photographed and hand fed, a honking cacophony of flapping white wings and outstretched necks. The road bends round into Mistley, and immediately passes the Mistley towers, two matching monuments that stand above the ancient gravestones in the railed churchyard. They may now look like a rich man's fantastical folly, but they still provide notable navigation landmarks. They were built by Richard Rigby as part of his church, the main church having long since collapsed and vanished from between the towers.

Rigby was a local landowner and MP, his father had made a fortune from the South Sea Bubble, and Rigby himself became Paymaster General for the king's forces. With his wealth he had developed the family home into a magnificent hall with extensive landscaped gardens, and the church was a part of his grandiose plan to turn Mistley into a fashionable spa resort, which he fondly hoped would rival Bath. Sadly Rigby went bankrupt, his church was later demolished, and the towers and the elegant white swan fountain in the centre of the town are poignant reminders of Rigby's dream.

However, the Mistley Quays, also built by the Rigby family, are still the heart of the port and are regularly visited by quite large ships from the Baltic. The extensive maltings which are passed on the way out of the town were also built by the Rigby family in the 1850s and are still in operation.

The Stour rolls on in a broad tidal ebb and flow to Harwich, glimpsed here and there across fields and gently rolling hedgerows from the narrow road that passes through Bradfield and Ramsey. At Bradfield the pretty little white-washed, red-roofed church of St Lawrence stands on a corner. Even the tower is two-tone, red-brick on top of smooth grey concrete. Harwich is the ancient port at the mouth of the estuary, although, before you reach it you will pass the modern new ferry terminal at Parkeston Quay, where the sleek white passenger ships set sail to France and Holland. However,

The Mistley towers, all that remains of the church that once stood between them.

Harwich Quay, with the tall cranes of Felixstowe docks on the far side of the estuary.

it is the old, stoutly-timbered Ha'penny Pier which holds a more enduring charm. It was built in 1883 as the ticket office for coastal paddle steamers, and later the harbour ferry. The ferry from Landguard Point still calls here, along with a variety of fishing boats and yachts. It is also a splendid viewing point to watch large ships and the occasional red-sailed barge going past.

In the twelfth century Harwich was a walled mediaeval town with a castle. The walls and castle have gone, but the ancient grid pattern of the old streets remains, many of them with fine old houses that were re-faced during the prosperous Georgian period. Some were the homes of wealthy sea captains, and one was the home of Christopher Jones, the master of the *Mayflower*, which carried the Pilgrim Fathers to America in 1620. The *Mayflower* was also built here in Harwich, and a fascinating exhibition tells the full story on the Ha'penny Pier. The Electric Palace cinema, the oldest unaltered purpose-built cinema in the country, is also worth a visit. It is fully restored and still shows films, but even between performances the splendid, soft green pargeting garlands, on its pristine white Dutch gable façade, makes a picture of its own.

Harwich was always an important maritime centre, and its fortunes ebbed and flowed like the tides of the Stour itself with the twin boons of war and trade. Those who were not navy men or honest merchants often thrived on the more clandestine business of smuggling, and many of those fine old houses have inter-connecting cellars to allow the free passage of men and contraband goods. There are two lighthouses here, the Low Lighthouse on the promenade between the sea and the spacious green, and across the green the High Lighthouse, a slender, 90ft, nine-sided brown brick

Harwich green, the High Lighthouse and the church spire.

tower. The first is now a museum, and the latter a private residence, but when they were in use the two lights in alignment told mariners that it was time to turn into the harbour mouth.

The final showpiece here is the massive, circular redoubt fort, built in Napoleonic times to protect the naval yard and the estuary mouth. The redoubt is 200ft in diameter, with walls 3ft thick and surrounded by a deep, dry moat. It was originally armed with ten 24-pounder cannons, but despite several upgrades of its armament it has never fired a shot in anger. Perhaps its formidable, solid and menacing presence was enough to keep all its enemies at bay.

Opposite, on the Suffolk side, is the giant container port of Felixstowe, so here is the perfect place to simply stop and admire the wide views across the estuary; and to watch the passing ships, large and small, that still glide slowly by.

Now that we have reached the sea we have come to the end of our journey along the Stour, but this delightful corner of Essex still has much to offer. Inland are the Tendring villages, and along the Essex Sunshine Coast are some of the finest holiday beaches in the county, curving from Dovercourt down to Clacton-on-Sea.

Harwich sits side-by-side with Dovercourt, which is the older town of the two. Traces of prehistoric settlement have been found here, including bronze axe heads. Today the town is a small but popular seaside resort, with safe sandy beaches and all the usual holiday shops selling buckets and spades, colourful inflatables, ice creams and fish and chips. After soaking up all the history and culture of the Harwich Maritime Trail, Dovercourt is the ideal neighbour where children can play and adults can relax.

Then the coast is broken up by the maze of creeks and channels of the Naze and the Walton Backwaters. Here you can see spectacular views from the top of the 86ft high, octagonal Navigational Tower which is now open to the public for the first time in over 280 years. Built in 1720, its spiral staircase winds up through eight floors before you emerge on top with the wind in your hair, with all of the backwaters and much of Essex and parts of Suffolk spread out far below. On a good sailing day the sea will be filled with racing white sails from the Walton Yacht Club.

Walton itself is another small but charming seaside resort, with good beaches and the second longest pier in England. The sea fishing from the far end is said to be excellent, and always attracts a dedicated flock of anglers. The town itself is one of small narrow streets and lovely old shops If you go up Old Pier Street and cross the High Street into Mill Lane you will find yourself walking past a high grass embankment towards the clustered masts of the Yacht Club. Here you will find the flavour of old maritime Walton, with boats and boatyards lying on either side of the entrance to the Walton Channel which winds its way through marsh and mudflats to the Naze and the sea.

Below Walton is Frinton, and a great expanse of grass-topped cliffs overlooking seemingly endless beaches, the safe smooth sands divided by long wooden breakwaters. In high summer, especially at weekends, the greensward on top of the cliffs is covered with holiday-makers, flying kites, playing cricket, or just picnicking or lazing in the sun. The beaches below are equally packed, although with so much space there is always room for everybody.

The golden sands sweep on to Clacton, undoubtedly the queen of this particular holiday coast. Clacton is unashamedly modern, and totally dedicated to providing the perfect seaside holiday. It has cliffs and gardens and promenades, and all the amusements, slot machines and funfairs you could wish for. Many of them are packed into the pier, pulsating with fun, laughter and noise, and reached by a road which dips under an elegant Venetian bridge.

If it is history you want, go to Harwich, for some genteel peace and quiet, but in this part of the world if you want good, hearty, full-bodied entertainment then it has to be Clacton. The major annual events here include Clacton Carnival Week, the Clacton Air Show, and Clacton Jazz Festival.

To complete a circular journey back to the Stour, head inland for Tendring, the tiny, scattered village in the heart of this agricultural corner of Essex between the Stour and the Colne. Tendring gives the district its name, derived from the Tendring Hundred, which refers to an ancient method of dividing up these rich farmlands between families. This is a gentle landscape, of cornfields and rape fields, farmhouses and barns, woods and hedgerows.

The villages are small and charming, full of cosy cottages and comfortable pubs, and each one with a noteworthy church close to its heart. The elegant spire of Tendring St Edmund's parish church can be seen for miles, while St Mary's in Great Bentley stands on the corner of the largest village green in England.

Ardleigh is the most western of the Tendring villages, with a charming group of sixteenth and seventeenth-century cottages grouped around another fine church. From here it is only a few miles back to Dedham and the Stour and the circle is complete.

CHAPTER THREE

THE BORDER RIVERS

The borders of the county of Essex are almost entirely made up of water. The ragged eastern edge is girdled by the sea. To the south is the broad flow of the Thames, and to the north the long, wandering valley of the Stour. To the east, separating Essex from Middlesex and Hertfordshire, are the gentle north to south valleys of the Stort and the Lee.

The Stort first appears as a gentle stream that flows through charming Clavering, where the old lane that leads down past the converted guildhall to the churchyard is said to be one of the most photographed and painted spots in all of Essex. Behind the church is the moated castle site where the Saxon Lord of the Manor, Robert Fitzwymark, built his stronghold before the Normans came. Nothing is left now, but the fact that a castle once stood here suggests that the Stort was not always such a small and sleepy trickle.

Clavering is a cluster of small village greens, with an ancient farm or cottage at almost every twist and

Clavering, the lane leading to the Old guildhall and the church, is a favourite with both photographers and artists.

Canal boats still linger in the shade at Bishop's Stortford.

turn. The Stort leaves it to wind merrily along to Manuden, which is another delightful village in which to linger. The church tower nestles comfortably among mature trees and thatched roofs, and away from the main roads there is an air of peace and rural calm.

Stansted Mountfitchet comes next, the site of another castle, this one a popular re-creation site with a palisade enclosing an extensive mediaeval village. Stansted has five churches, including the splendid red-brick St John's Church, centre placed behind delightful lawns and flower gardens. In spring they are bright with daffodils. There is also a restored-brick tower windmill, built in 1877, which was in continuous service until 1910. It still has most of its original machinery and is said to be one of the best preserved mills in England. As always in any Essex village, there is also a variety of fascinating ancient buildings, shops, and public houses, ranging from half timbered Tudor through Georgian and Victorian.

Nearby Stansted Airfield was used by heavy bombers during the Second World War and had one of the longest runways in Great Britain. Almost inevitably it was developed afterwards into London's third airport, and is still expanding.

Through more pastoral fields and farmlands the river reaches Bishop's Stortford, where it becomes the county border. Bishop's Stortford is on the Hertfordshire side of the river, but as the head of the old Stort Navigation we can hardly ignore it. Several Roman roads once crossed here, and slowly the first settlement evolved into a thriving market town around a once important ford over the river.

There was a castle here in 1060, when both the town and castle were sold to the Bishop of London. The castle was later destroyed by King John, who briefly seized the

The Black Lion and the town centre of Bishop's Stortford.

town during a dispute in the thirteenth century. John later rebuilt the castle, but in the end, time claimed it. Now only the foundations remain in the form of the castle mound rising up in a grass-covered hill in the Castle Gardens beside the river.

The town also has some lovely old inns, the Black Lion which dates back to the sixteenth century, and the fifteenth-century Boars Head on Wind Hill. Also on top of Wind Hill, overlooking the town stands St Michael's Church, again built mainly in the fifteenth century. The church tower and its crowning spire were added in 1812. On the wall of the north aisle there is a memorial to Cecil Rhodes, the founder of Rhodesia, now Zimbabwe, who was the son of a former vicar and was born here in 1853.

Until the eighteenth century, the Stort was too meandering and shallow to be of much commercial use, but then the Stort Navigation was constructed south of the town to link up with the Lee. The river was widened and re-routed and fifteen wooden locks constructed to enable barges laden with grain and malt barley to be taken down to bustling London to provide bread and beer, and the town of Bishop's Stortford prospered. Incidentally, it was the town which gave its name to the river, and not the other way around.

The river drifts on, curving west to slip past Harlow, and providing some lovely river walks and scenic landscapes in the 64 acres of Harlow Town Park. The town itself could be easily mistaken by the passing stranger for a network of traffic-clogged by-passes and roundabouts, but find your way through the outlying industrial estates and into the ultra-modern town centre and you will be pleasantly surprised.

The multi-storey car park leads into a magnificent shopping mall, a dedicated cathedral to commerce, and beyond are more lively large shops set in paved pedestrian streets and squares, all liberally sprinkled with modernistic stone and bronze statues and sculptures.

There are extensive water gardens laid out in three levels in front of the civic centre. The lower level is a maze of lawns and square gardens divided by patios and walkways, with plenty of places to simply sit or lie in the sun. The second level is a long, narrow water feature, with a back wall of blue tiles and a series of Mexican style panel sculptures in alternating squares and sun circles. The third and upper level is another long pool with a bronze boar and a bronze cormorant. At the far end a nude woman, again in green bronze, shyly raises her arms to shield her face.

Harlow is, of course, a new town, specifically planned and designed to accommodate London's overspill, and an obelisk memorial monument in the High Street, close to the modern market place, commemorates the long building period from 1947 to 1980.

The river wanders east, curving past Roydon and then swinging south again to where it eventually joins the Lee at Fields Weir. Near here, at Nazeing, is where Boudicca, Queen of the Ancient Britons, fought her last battle against the disciplined

The water gardens are a central feature at Harlow.

might of the Roman Army. Here too, at Nazeingbury, was the site of some of the communal graves dug to accommodate the bodies of the plague victims shipped upstream from the heart of London some 1,300 years later.

The Lee valley becomes the River Lee Country Park for the next stage of its journey. On the Essex side of the river there was once the vast sprawl of ancient Epping Forest, the 60,000 acre hunting grounds of a long succession of Saxon, Norman and Tudor kings. It is much curtailed and encroached upon now, perhaps only a tenth of its former glory, but still an impressive oasis of green glades, great oaks, beech and hornbeams. It is no longer a dark and dangerous place, haunted by outlaws and highwaymen, and can now be happily explored by a maze of footpaths, cycle paths, and bridleways.

What is left of the forest now is mainly along either side of the A104, entered from the north through the long town of Epping. The first sight of Epping is an attractive one. The new civic offices rise above the long green, with a handsome clock tower which makes it look more like an ultra-modern church. Up through the busy High Street and market and there you will find the real church, the splendid grey stone tower of the Church of St John the Baptist, with its distinctive wood-cased clock projecting over the pavement. The church was built in three stages on the site of an earlier chapel beginning in 1889, and the clock was added in 1909. Of all the treasures inside the most striking is the elegant dark oak tracery of the rood screen that dominates the entrance to the Choir.

As you leave the town there is one last high-rise landmark, the tall, red-brick Victorian water tower. Then you are passing through the forest. At the southern

Two symbols of Epping, the town sign and the Victorian water tower.

end, just before Chingford is the location of Queen Elizabeth's hunting lodge. It was actually built in 1543 for King Henry VIII, as a grandstand to watch the deer hunting, in the days when there were large herds of wild deer and the king's archers hunted with longbows or crossbows. Now it is preserved as a tourist attraction and a reminder of those grand Tudor days of Merry Olde England, when lords and ladies, courtiers and minstrels, all gathered on the greensward to watch the thrill of the hunt

However, we have strayed a little and must move east again to Waltham to rejoin the Lee. The forest once stretched this far, and was once known as Waltham Forest before it became Epping Forest. Much of the ancient Abbey Church dates back to the twelfth century. The town that is clustered around it also has many old timber-framed buildings. The old Welsh Harp pub beside the market place, with the church tower rising beyond its slanting red roof, makes a particularly pleasing picture.

History was made here. Harold, the last Saxon King of England, is said to be buried under a grave slab behind the church, and the full story is related in chapter five. Today there are still traces of the cloisters and the old Abbey gateway in the Abbey

The Welsh Harp with the tower of Waltham Abbey behind.

Gardens behind the church. There are charming rose gardens, and a small ancient stone footbridge, still known as Harold's bridge, crossing the Cornmill stream that leads into the Lee. The Cornmill Meadows nearby are now a dragonfly sanctuary, where with time and patience on a good summer's day you may be able to count up to twenty-one different types of native species.

A more unusual attraction is the site of the Royal Gunpowder Mills, established in 1665. The site was originally a fulling mill set up to produce cloth on the Millhead stream by the monks of Waltham Abbey. It was sold and converted to producing vegetable oil, and then to the manufacture of gunpowder. The mills expanded and in 1787 they were purchased by the Crown.

Explosives and armaments were developed here, helping to win the Battle of Waterloo and forging three centuries of history as the British Empire expanded across the globe. The First World War caused a huge upsurge in both research and production and the explosive in the Bouncing Bomb that destroyed the Ruhr dams was developed here in the 1940s. In 1943 the mills were closed and production moved to the West Country, away from the reach of German bombs, but in 1945 the facility re-opened to become a research centre that helped to develop fuel for rocket engines until it closed in 1991. Now the 172 acre site, with more than a score of historic buildings, hosts living history events and guided tours, and the network of surrounding canals and woodlands have become a nature reserve.

At Waltham we are at the southern end of the Lee Valley Country Park, a valley maze of waterways, lakes and flooded gravel pits that stretch north almost to the point where the Stort and the Lee join their waters. This is a ramblers' paradise of themed walks, with such an abundance of plant and wildlife that it has been designated a site of special scientific interest.

To the south, the Lee runs down into the vast city sprawl of London, through Tottenham, Walthamstow and Hackney marshes. London's waterways, excluding the Thames, include over 80 miles of linked canals and natural rivers, most of them hidden from the main roads. The Lee alone has 10,000 acres of regional parklands along its course, an artery of rich green threading into the heart of the city.

At Blackwall, just below the power station, the River Lee loses its identity to turn into the wider Thames. Both of the rivers we have followed are now devoted mainly to leisure, a world of rowing clubs and marinas, towpath walks and other riverside pursuits. On the upper reaches there are havens for birds and butterflies, insects, wild flowers and small mammals. Our first little stream which began north of Clavering will eventually have circled almost two sides of the county before finally becoming lost in the English Channel.

CHAPTER FOUR

IN DEFENCE OF ESSEX

It is a sad fact of history that wherever people put down roots and settle they will inevitably have to defend themselves and their holdings. Way back in the Stone Age, the first Neanderthal family groups probably built walls of defensive rocks across the mouths of their caves. Later, earthworks would be built up to make a defensive site, and finally a wooden palisade to construct the first Iron Age hilltop forts. Then the Romans came and built many of their forts on the existing native sites.

Finally, the greatest robbers of all came along with the army of William the Conqueror and his land-hungry Norman knights. They took the whole country, shared out the lands, and then set to building their own massive castle walls to defend it all against the dispossessed and each other.

At Pleshey, Geoffrey de Mandeville took over the lordship of some 12,000 acres of prime Essex land, and there built up the ancient earthworks that may well have been started in prehistoric times, building his huge motte and bailey castle on top. Nothing remains now except the massive, semi-circular grass bank, which once supported the outer wall, half embracing the great circular mound where the castle keep would have towered high above.

At Saffron, Walden, de Mandeville built a second castle, where some impressive ruins still remain, a few flint-rubble walls of the old keep, and a small tower added later in 1796, to enable a signal beacon to be lit in the event of a French invasion. However, many of the castle stones had already been plundered in the mid-thirteenth century to help build the foundations of the new church.

At Chipping Ongar, there was a great Norman castle, built by Richard de Lucy, but that too was later demolished in the reign of Queen Elizabeth I. There were more castles at Newport, Rayleigh, Clavering and Great Canfield. At least fourteen Norman castles were built in Essex, and most of them have vanished or diminished to a mere trace of rubble or earthworks over the course of time.

These grey flint walls are all that remain of the castle at Saffron Walden.

One superb exception is at Castle Hedingham, where the magnificent keep with its 12ft-thick walls, faced with mellowed Barnack stone, rise up to 110ft. It was built by Aubrey de Vere, one of the richest and most powerful of the Norman nobles, and one of the few who could afford to build in stone rather than timber. The de Veres became the Earls of Oxford, and one of the most important families in the land.

In 1215, the Third Earl of Oxford was one of the twenty-six barons who forced King John to sign the Magna Carta. For this he was excommunicated when the balance of power swung back in John's favour, and with the other barons he offered the English Crown to the king of France. In the turmoil that followed, Castle Hedingham was besieged twice, first by the vengeful King John of England, and then by the King of France when the castle was retaken. It was only after the death of King John, when the barons made peace with Henry III, the new King of England, that the Earls of Oxford were returned to the fold and the king's grace.

Today Hedingham Castle still shows evidence of its past glories and turbulent history. The spectacular arched banqueting hall in the great keep is 28ft wide and rises to a height of 20ft. It is easy to imagine it filled with feasting knights and ladies, with minstrels and jugglers playing, and great wolfhounds chewing bones beneath the laden tables. If your imagination needs help there are frequent mediaeval re-creation days when you can see knights jousting at tournament, or the castle once again defying a siege.

To complete the picture of mediaeval Essex you should also visit Stansted Mountfitchet. Here, soon after the Conquest, Robert Gernon, the Duke of Boulogne, built his castle on a defended site that could also trace its history back through the Vikings, Saxons and Romans. Nothing remains of Gernon's original twelfth-century construction. That too was attacked and in this case demolished in 1215 by the angry King John. However, 700 years on it has all been rebuilt as faithfully as possible to give a fascinating reconstruction of life at all levels in those harsh days.

A defensive palisade surrounds the mediaeval village at Stansted Mountfitchet.

The War Memorial stands outside the gates to the park and Colchester Castle.

A complete Norman village is enclosed within the stockade walls that stand again on top of huge earthworks. In the score of cramped, thatch-roofed cottages you will find the blacksmith, the carpenter, the pottery-maker, the brewer, the weaver, and the candle-maker, and all of those tiny industries that were the mainstay of mediaeval life. On a more sombre note you can see the gallows and the prison hole. Except for the ducks that float idly on the ponds and the deer and chickens that roam freely, all of the characters and images are snapshots frozen in time.

Colchester Castle stands in the heart of the ancient town, built in 1079 by Eudo Dapifer, the steward and one of the chief confidants of William the Conqueror. It was built on the platform of the great Roman temple dedicated to that earlier Conqueror of Britain, the Roman Emperor Claudius, and so contains more history than almost any other site in England.

In 1216, Colchester Castle joined the list of strongholds besieged by King John in the Barons' War, and in 1648 the town and castle were besieged again by the Parliamentary Army during the English Civil War. After seventy-seven days the Royalist defenders were starved into surrender, and the two commanders were shot by the north wall of the castle. A memorial stone marks the spot where the executions took place.

Today the chipped and rugged stone walls, topped by red roof tiles, can glow a gentle orange when the sunlight is of the right quality, almost like a Tuscan monastery. The castle is now a museum and is surrounded by peaceful landscaped gardens and the tranquillity of the Castle Park. Its days of excitement and violence are over.

The last of the great Norman castles was a shift back to the more traditional concerns of defence, to guard against the foreign invader. The building of Hadleigh Castle was begun by Hubert de Burgh in 1231 on high ground to overlook Canvey Island and the Thames. However, Hubert fell from grace and so the castle was taken over and completed by his King, Henry III. Later it was strengthened by Edward III to protect London from a possible French invasion up the Thames. When that danger, passed the money for the upkeep of the castle dwindled until over the next two centuries the mighty walls slowly crumbled away. The ruins that remain are haunting and splendid, where now only doves play at ghosts in the fragments, but they still command a fine view across the river.

The fears and real dangers of French aggression waxed and waned, and defence of the Thames again became a priority with the later Kings of England. The middle of the seventeenth century was the great age of New World exploitation, and the seaboard nations of Europe were all in fierce competition for the spoils. The Essex scenario was no longer one of English Kings and barons fighting each other, but the outward-looking fears of new foreign invasions by France, Holland, or Spain.

Musketeers had now replaced archers, and the much more devastating cannon had replaced the old, creaking, hand-pushed siege engine. Tall stone keep towers and high-standing walls were obsolete against hard-hitting cannonballs, so the next generation of defences were totally different.

The monumental Water Gate is the Thames-side entrance to Tilbury Fort.

Artillery pieces inside
Tilbury Fort.

From the massive walls
of Harwich Redoubt
Fort, Second World War
artillery still guards the
river mouth into the
Orwell and the Stour.

Tilbury Fort was built in the late seventeenth century, where it could guard the narrowing stretch of the Thames just before it reaches London. It was constructed on a massive five-pointed star pattern so that each wall could be covered by fire from another, and surrounded on its three landward sides by a double moat. The earthworks were able to absorb enemy artillery, and the fort's own gunpowder magazines were buried deep underground. Its gun lines faced the river, where more batteries on the opposite bank could provide a murderous crossfire. If Drake had not stopped the Spanish Armada at sea, then Tilbury Fort would have been London's last line of defence.

Over the next two centuries a whole string of forts were constructed along both sides of the Thames. In Victorian times a new wave of re-fortification began to meet the new threat of the first French iron-clad warships. A major construction at this time was Coalhouse Fort, again built at Tilbury on the site of earlier defensive works on the Thames coast. This was an entirely new design to meet the threat of the times, a casement fortress which meant that twenty-two gigantic guns were housed in large vaulted rooms with armour-plated fronts. Underneath the fortress was an extensive magazine tunnel system to store the shells and move them quickly to the artillery. This was London's new, front-line defence.

Further north the second major Essex anchorage at the mouth of the Stour saw the construction of the Harwich Redoubt Fort in 1810. Surrounded by a great dry moat 20ft in depth, this huge circular fortification again mounted its guns to cover the mouth of the rivers Orwell and Stour. The fort was another massive structure with impressive firepower, built to keep Napoleon at bay.

Tilbury Fort was still garrisoned during the First World War, and Harwich and Coalhouse Forts last saw service during the Second World War. After that the preparations for the defence of Essex went completely underground. Top-secret blast-proof bunkers were built at Mistley and at Kelvedon Hatch during the height of the Cold War. From here the top military commanders and the Government would have attempted to direct whatever might have been left of the county, the country and the war, in the event of a nuclear exchange between Russia and the West.

Mercifully they were never needed. Both became tourist attractions, although Mistley is now closed down. However, the Kelvedon Hatch bunker is still open to visitors, as are the castles at Hedingham, Colchester and Stansted Mountfitchet, and the forts at Tilbury, Coalhouse and Harwich. All are well worth a visit if you are interested in any aspect of the historical defence of Essex.

CHAPTER FIVE

ESSEX ABBEYS – GLORY IN STONE

Religion was the great mainstay of mediaeval life, the underpinning strength of hope and faith which was probably the only comfort in many otherwise harsh and miserable lives. The poor had their parish churches, while the rich paid penance to save their souls in pilgrimage crusades to the Holy Land, or used their wealth to found magnificent abbeys and priories.

Before the Reformation the parish church simply followed the Catholic teachings. However, there were around fifty established religious houses in Essex which were dedicated to one or other of the great monastic orders that developed into their own closed communities committed to worship and prayer. Many of them, due to royal and noble patronage, became concentrations of great wealth and power, some of them holding thousands of acres of land.

The great riverside abbey at Barking, St John's Abbey at Colchester, and the priories at Hatfield and Earls Colne were all Benedictine monasteries. The Benedictines followed the rule of Saint Benedict of Nursia, who founded the first twelve monasteries at Subiaco near Rome in the sixth century. His rule of life incorporated communal living, physical labour, worship and prayer, and the distribution of food and alms to the poor. It became the model for all monastic orders and revitalised the concept of monastic life all over Europe.

In 1140 King Stephen built the abbey at Coggeshall and gave it to the Cistercians, who were a breakaway order from the Benedictines. They regarded their brother monks in the original order as having become lax and undisciplined. Probably they had good cause, as they were not the only reformed Benedictine movement. The great Burgundian abbey at Cluny in France had also seen the need to tighten up the Benedictine rule, and their new Cluniac Order also spread to Essex and the priory at Prittlewell.

At Coggeshall, the huge Grange Barn that was the abbey storehouse is almost all that remains. However, Prittlewell Priory still stands, preserved as a museum to its past in the charming setting of the rose-splashed Priory Park and Gardens at Southend.

Left: An epitaph for 1066. A simple grave slab at Waltham Abbey marks the spot where the remains of the ill-fated King Harold are believed to lie.

Below: Waltham Abbey Church from the Abbey Gardens.

The Augustines were the Order of the Hermit Friars of Saint Augustine of Hippo, who kept to strict rules of poverty and saw their mission as one of preaching and tending the sick. Their code was to 'Live together in harmony, being of one heart and one mind on The Way to God.' The magnificent abbey at Waltham and the priories at Leeze, St Osyth, and St Botolph's Priory at Colchester were all Augustinian monasteries.

However, they too had their dissidents. At Chelmsford there was a Dominican Friary, following the order established by Saint Dominic, who had seen fit to make some adaptation to the Augustinian rule. The Dominicans wanted to be free of any bond to any particular order, so that they could concentrate on the prime task of preaching wherever it was needed, and so they created a new order of their own.

Beeleigh Abbey, the Monastery of St Mary and St Nicholas at the head of the Blackwater near Maldon, is now privately owned. It was founded in 1170 by Sir Robert de Mantel, and was the only house of the Premonstratensian Order to be sited in Essex. This particular order was founded by Saint Norbet of Prémontré in Northern France, and they saw their prime duty in the singing of the Divine Offices. They preferred to stay more aloof from the common people, and favoured more remote and isolated locations for their houses, away from the distractions and temptations of towns.

The general difference between the orders was mainly in the emphasis or priority of the various aspects of their role, should a monk's life be devoted to healing the sick, preaching, or private prayer. However, life inside a monastery or nunnery followed a basic pattern that would start in the very early hours of the morning. There would usually be at least eight hours of divine services, when prayers would be offered and the rituals of psalms, chants, hymns and anthems would be sung. The actual work in the kitchens and the fields would be left to lay brethren, except in the poorer houses. In the great abbeys, the time was given to silent reading, or the creation and copying of religious manuscripts.

There was always a fine abbey or priory church on one side of the central cloisters, on the other three sides would be the living quarters and latrines, the dormitories where the monks slept and the refectory where they ate their simple meals. After their vows were taken it was understood that the initiates would spend the rest of their lives in this holy environment.

Barking Abbey was perhaps the richest in Essex. It was built in AD 666, razed by the Danes who pillaged its treasures and burned to death all the nuns in their own church in AD 870, and was rebuilt one hundred years later in AD 970. Its abbess was created as a peer of the realm, the rank always passing through aristocratic families and including three queens and two princesses. At this level, in one of the great ecclesiastical seats of power, the abbot or abbess would be spared much of the tedium of monastic life. His or her role would revolve instead around power politics, administration, and the entertainment of passing kings.

Today the small river port that was mediaeval Barking, the abbey and its lands, have almost all been obliterated by the advance of Greater London. All that remains is one bell tower, which was used as a fire and curfew bell. Its value to the town in this role meant that it escaped the general destruction of the Dissolution.

The unfortunate nuns of Barking Abbey were not the only ones to fall prey to Viking raiders. In AD 633, more war galleys had sailed up the Chelm to where Osyth, the daughter of the East Saxon king, was the prioress in the nunnery established by her father. When the pagan ruffians tried to force the terrified nuns to renounce their

The ruins of the old gateway at Waltham Abbey.

Christian faith, Osyth stepped bravely forward to confront them. She was beheaded on the spot, but the legend says that she picked up her own head and carried it back to the nunnery chapel. She was later canonised as St Osyth, and St Osyth's Priory grew into the splendour of which much still remains today. The magnificent three-storey gatehouse, built in the fifteenth century, topped with battlements and faced with dressed flint, still shields the surviving abbey buildings and gardens from general view.

The religious houses were a prime and easy target for these seaborne marauders, but at least they could recover and be rebuilt. However, when Henry VIII became greedy for their wealth and lands, there was no reprieve. The Dissolution meant that most of the great religious houses were demolished, their vast land estates, their wealth and power confiscated for ever. Generally the occupants were more mercifully treated, provided they left quietly, but there were exceptions. The abbot of St John's Abbey at Colchester resisted and was tried for treason and executed.

Now only a single gateway remains of St John's, although nearby there are some much more impressive ruins of St Botolph's Priory. This had been the first Augustinian Priory in England, built by the Normans who had borrowed most of the red-brick from the constructions of the Romans. Here the great crumbled stone archways of the west font still stand, a testament to the magnificence and durability of the original building.

A few of the abbey churches escaped destruction, where they are still in use as parish churches today. The most splendid example of these is the 1,000-year-old Abbey

Above: At Colchester stand the magnificent ruins of St Botolph's Priory.

Right: The magnificent flint-faced gateway of St Osyth's Priory.

Prittlewell Priory is now a museum in the Priory Gardens at Southend.

Church at Waltham. The huge nave with its massive incised pillars and Norman archways, combined with its high painted ceiling and surrounded by beautiful stained-glass windows, must surely rate as one of the most glorious surviving examples of mediaeval religious architecture.

Waltham has a long history. The first timber church was built here in the seventh century, and then the first stone church around AD 790. In AD 1030, a carpenter in Somerset had a dream which directed him to dig into a certain hill, and there he discovered a life-size black stone crucifix which was exquisitely carved with the figure of Christ. The figure was lifted on to an ox cart, and as though through a will of their own, the oxen hauled it to Waltham. So goes the legend of the Waltham Holy Cross. So here, on what was then the edge of the great Epping Forest, Harold Godwinson, then the Earl of Wessex but later to become King Harold, built and consecrated a college for twelve secular canons.

Harold prayed here on his way to the fateful Battle of Hastings, and later his body was brought back here to rest. His statue, sword in hand, stands in a niche at the south-west corner of the present church, and his grave is marked by a simple slab behind the east wall.

Henry II raised the status of Harold's church to an Augustinian Abbey, which was to become one of the greatest in the land. Even Henry VIII, who began the Dissolution of the Monasteries in the 1520s, spared Waltham Abbey until 1542, when it became the last English religious house to be dissolved.

We are fortunate that the Abbey Church remains.

CHAPTER SIX

TALL TOWERS AND WHITE SAILS

The white sails of a windmill, out-flung against a June-blue sky or a red-gold sunset, are all part of the nostalgic essence of rural Essex. Often peeping over a wooded hilltop, or from behind a sleepy church tower or some cosily thatched cottage, they invoke a haunting image of a golden yesterday.

The earliest windmills first appeared in ancient Persia around the seventh century AD, and from there spread into France and then England around the eleventh and twelfth centuries. They were the high technology of their time, harnessing wind power to drive large circular stones that ground corn to make bread. The earliest structures were the post mills, where the entire windmill could be rotated around a central post to bring the sails into the prevailing wind. Tower mills came later, more solidly built of brick, with a rotating cap on top, turned by a fan tail, which also caught the wind to move the sails into a position where again they could be revolved.

All over England, windmills, and water mills, where great wheels were turned by the natural flow of a stream or river, were adapted to a variety of tasks. They could be used for pumping and irrigation, and virtually anything that could be facilitated by the power of a turning wheel. However, they are primarily remembered for the job of grinding corn. The miller, resplendent in his apron and in his white coating of flour dust, was one of the most important men in any mediaeval community, as vital to its existence as the blacksmith, the Lord of the Manor, or the priest.

In their heyday there were thousands of wind and watermills all over England and hundreds of them in Essex alone. The vast majority of windmills have disappeared but most of those that remain are lovingly preserved and restored to their former external glory, many of them also in full internal working order. Essex has some of the finest examples in the land, all of them well worth a visit.

The oldest windmill in the county is at Great Bardfield, dating back to around 1660. You will find it hidden by trees and hedgerows up a minor road on the edge of the village. During its long history it has been converted into a house, reverted back into a

Great Bardfield tower mill dates from around 1660, and is probably the oldest in Essex.

working mill for almost two centuries more, and then reconverted into a private house again. It lost its sails in the great storm of 1987 that thrashed the entire landscape of southern and eastern England, but these have since been replaced with a non-working set. It still looks like a windmill.

The tallest windmill is at Rayleigh, built in 1809, just north of Southend. Its cap stands 60ft above the old castle mound, sharing the skyline with the tower of Holy Trinity Church.

The prettiest well, that has to be a matter of personal choice, and there are plenty to choose from. John Webb's sturdy old red-brick tower mill standing proud above the surrounding fields at Thaxted has to be a strong contender, but so is the smaller, white-timbered post mill at Finchingfield. Its central position, in this small, charming Essex village, gives it that extra appeal.

Many mills have been moved during the course of their lifetime, for one reason or another. The Bocking post mill, just outside of Braintree, dates from around 1721, but it was moved eastwards and up the hill by about 170 yards in the 1800s, when some newly-built cottages blocked it off from the essential wind. On the round brick tower base large, white letters still paint out the words STEAM AND WINDMILL, GRIST GROUND ON THE SHORTEST NOTICE. OATS CRUSHED, RETAILING DONE.

Some Essex mills are privately owned, a few converted into private dwellings and some are cared for by Essex County Council. Most of these are open to the public on set days, usually on one Sunday of each summer month from April to September. However, they are all open on National Windmills Weekend, which is always the second weekend in May.

To find out more about the work of the Trust and the mammoth task of keeping this vital part of Essex heritage alive, I talked to Geoff Wood, the Mill Support Officer for Heritage Conservation with Essex County Council. We met over coffee in

Chelmsford County Hall, where I found a man with an undisguised passion for his job, happy to tell me everything there was to know about windmills.

Geoff explained:

In 1860 there were 280 windmills in Essex. By 1932 there were less than forty left, and by 1950 less then twenty. Because the windmills were disappearing so fast from our landscape, Essex decided as a matter of policy that it was necessary to preserve what was left as a valuable part of our culture and countryside.

Now there are twenty-two recognisable mills left in the county, although many of them are converted into houses or used for storage. My department cares for four windmills, the tide mill at Thorington, the water mill at Sible Hedingham, and the steam mill at Beeleigh, so basically our portfolio includes at least one of each. All four of our windmills are fully restored, and the three at Aythorpe Roding, Stock, and Mountnessing are all capable of grinding corn. We start them up at least once a year to keep the machinery going.

Geoff works with a team of three; himself, millwright Michael Hoyle and his assistant Graham Robinson. Together they have restored and maintain the county portfolio of wind and water mills, and also advise on the restoration and preservation of all the privately owned mills in the county.

Bocking Windmill, also owned by Essex County Council, is one that has been moved from its original site, probably because it became shielded from the wind by cottages built in the early 1800s.

Geoff continued cheerfully:

As the Mills Officer, I have to wear about four different hats. I am responsible for the health and safety of all our visitors to the mills, for the training of the various support groups who operate the mills on our behalf on open days, looking after all the admin, and giving talks and tours to various groups and societies, not just about our own wind and water mills, but about all the mills in Essex.

We do all our own repairs and maintenance and because we have our own millwright the need to go to any outside contractors is very rare. We have our own workshops where we can fabricate most of the parts that we require, and then we fit them ourselves. We use only the original materials and we work using the original techniques. If the original part was a twelve inch by twelve inch oak post, then the replacement part will be a twelve inch by twelve inch oak post. There are no short cuts. And I think the county is probably unique among all the authorities in the country in that we seem to be the only one in which we are doing it all ourselves.

I asked him about the annual National Mills Weekend. Geoff replied promptly:

It's organised by the Society for the Protection of Ancient Buildings. It came about because they wanted to draw attention to the plight and condition of many of the nation's windmills, and to raise the profile and public awareness of windmills generally. In the first few years there were only a few hundred mills open, but the idea has taken hold and it's grown with every year. Last year on National Mills Weekend there were more than 700 mills open all across the country.

Mountnessing; a restored post mill constructed around 1807. It was bought by Essex County Council for 1s, and is now in full working order.

At all our mills we have groups of volunteers who act as guides to the general public on open days. That's not just National Mills Weekend, there's also the Heritage Weekend in September when all of our mills are open, and each mill is also open for one Sunday of each month. On a nice day we can get more than 100 people turn up to visit a windmill, and we have had them queuing out in the streets. You can only get twelve to fifteen people into a windmill at any one time, so it can be hard work to get them all through the mill to enjoy it.

There have been major restorations over the years, but having got the mills into restored condition the main task is with continuous maintenance and repairing the damage caused by adverse weather conditions. Geoff stressed:

Regular maintenance is essential. You have to wax them and grease them, and check, check, and double check, which saves money in the end. When they were built most of the cogging and most of the gearing was simply wedged into position, and most of the wedges are constantly wearing, or shrinking and expanding with humidity, so if you

neglect your maintenance you are simply storing up trouble for the future. Windmills are beautiful, but they are a job forever.

Geoff is a man who is very happy with his job. Seventy-five per cent of his time he is out of his office, physically working on the windmills, or showing people around. 'When you are walking around inside a windmill you are actually inside a machine,' he enthused. 'And they are such romantic machines. Newly married couples often come and have their wedding photographs taken in front of a windmill.'

Stock windmill, an early nineteenth-century tower mill with five floors, also owned by Essex County Council and fully restored to working order.

Left: John Webb's Windmill at Thaxted, standing tall in a field of yellow rape.

Below: Thorington Tide Mill, beautifully restored by Essex County Council, stands at the head of a small tributary of the Colne.

I went in search of some of Geoff's windmills. The splendid restored mill at Mountnessing was built in 1807, but a mill has stood on this site since the middle of the fifteenth century. The square, white clapboard body of the mill stands on a red-brick roundhouse, its broad sails soaring skyward. It was initially restored by Mountnessing Parish Council, and was then bought by Essex County Council for the sum of 1*s*.

Stock windmill is another beautiful old red-brick tower mill, the only survivor of three mills which once stood on Stock Common. Now it is closed in by trees and flanked with smart, modern bungalows. Like the mills at Mountnessing and Aythorpe Roding, it has been restored to working order.

Half way up the tower wall is a large black belt wheel, marking where it was driven by a steam engine in later years when steam became a more reliable alternative to the wind.

However, perhaps the most charming of Geoff's portfolio of mills is the unique nineteenth-century tide mill at Thorington on an inlet from the Colne estuary, the only survivor of one of the many similar mills that once lined the coastal creeks and rivers of the county. When the milling world went into decline after the 1850s, the tide mills disappeared, most of them being allowed to simply decay and collapse.

Thorington now is a tall, square timber building, sparkling in a new coat of brilliant white paint. It stands between a narrow creek running up to the massive water wheel, and a small, calm lake occupied by ducks and swans. In August there were background hills of farmland rolling up to the woodlands beyond, the fields golden with stubble and bales of rolled straw. The mill itself is again restored to full working order.

The last working mill in Essex was the smock mill at Terling, near Hatfield Peverel. Sadly the miller, Herbert Bonner, who had operated the mill safely for the previous fifty years, was killed in a tragic accident in 1950. He was caught in the machinery and crushed to death, always an occupational hazard for millers, and that put the final end to commercial milling in Essex. This was the same windmill where the comedian Will Hay was whirled around on the sails in the film of *Oh Mister Porter*. Now there are no sails and the old mill body is a white painted annex to a private home.

The history of windmills can be both tragic and comic, but their enduring legacy is still in the warm glow of nostalgia which they invoke. No doubt the reality was not so idyllic, but we still tend to see windmills and the memories they evoke through rose-tinted glasses.

I shall leave the last word with Geoff, who said that, 'to imagine Finchingfield without its windmill would be like imagining Marilyn Monroe without her crown of glorious blonde hair. To imagine Thaxted without its windmill would be just unthinkable.' I had to agree with him, for the Essex countryside without its fascinating heritage of windmills just would not be the same.

CHAPTER SEVEN

WHERE TIME STANDS STILL

Most visitors to the top north-eastern corner of Essex will be exploring the much publicised delights of Saffron Waldon, the Jacobean elegance of the great house at Audley End, or the reconstructed Norman castle at Stansted Mountfitchet. Others will simply be hurrying direct to the contentious sprawl of modern Stansted Airport, intent on making a premature exit from Essex altogether.

However, for the truly discerning there is still more to see in these gentle landscapes that roll lazily up to the Cambridgeshire border. There are some charming little villages, each one a small oasis of Old World nostalgia where thatched cottages and ancient timbered buildings snuggle close around the solid, comforting towers of their mediaeval churches. Linked by pastoral farmlands and bird-rich hedgerows, there is often more here than immediately meets the eye.

A lovely sunny morning in the middle of a rare April heatwave was a good time to make a circular drive, passing under the M11 to where the hedgerows were white with the first May blossom and the fields bursting into the first flowers of yellow rape, a unique spring landscape of snow and gold.

Tucked up close against the border, almost as far east as it could get and still be in Essex, is the tiny village of Berden. Here stands the mellow, sun-baked Church of St Nicholas, faced with pebbles of uncut flint, with a red-tiled roof and a red-tiled pyramid roof on top of the tower. The church was dedicated at the beginning of the thirteenth century, but around the base of the tower and built into the flint-work you can find the edges of the red clay tiles that are said to have come from an even older Roman villa. However, the Romans were not the first to appreciate the delights of this beautiful corner of Essex. In 1907 a skeleton was found nearby in what archaeologists believe to have been a Bronze Age burial mound. The first men were probably here at least 4,000 years ago.

Inside the church hangs a lovingly stitched tapestry which was obviously done to celebrate the Millennium. The church itself was the central feature, with about twenty of the most striking buildings in the village grouped around it. In this timeless landscape it seems that nearly every other building in almost every village is ancient and listed.

In fact they are very proud of their heritage in this part of the world, and it seems that virtually every community was keen to celebrate this by doing something for the Millennium. In Clavering, they photographed every house and household in the village to create the Clavering Chronicle, a complete and permanent record of the village at the turn of the century. In tiny Arkesden they had done something very similar, which was to put together a book in which every building was photographed from the air.

The drive continued up the gentle valley of the River Stort to return to Clavering, a photographer's delight set in rolling farmlands and strung along the B1038 in a winding necklace of small ancient greens, with little clusters of mixed modern buildings and picturesque old country houses and cottages. To find it on the map, first locate Saffron Walden, and then look on the other side of the A11 towards the Hertfordshire border.

Church End is where the narrow road winds down past the ancient thatched and yellow plastered guildhall to the fourteenth-century church of St Clement and St Mary. There was an earlier church on this site, which may have been the chapel for the great Norman castle which once dominated Clavering. It was one of the first Norman castles in England, although all that remains now is the moat that once

Church End at Clavering, the old guildhall.

surrounded the central keep, and some traces of the mediaeval earthworks that still dictate the layout of the lanes and streets.

This is the old heart of the village. Some of the older houses date back to 1400, including the Fox and Hounds pub, and one, the Bury, goes back to 1300. The church was built between 1300 and 1500. There is also a United Reform Church, and a red-brick Methodist Chapel, both built in the 1800s, plus a couple of old mill towers dating back to the same period It is also one of the more fortunate rural villages which still has its school, a new supermarket and post office, as well as its two pubs. The other pub, The Cricketers, is owned by the father of TV chef Jamie Oliver, and is something of a gastronomic Mecca.

However, Clavering is not just a nostalgic pastiche of open greens, old lanes and a potted history of the evolution of cottages and houses. Clavering is alive and forward-looking, and in 1998 won the Essex Village of the Year Award for its community spirit, and was also the runner-up nationally. It was an award which gave a real feeling of pride within the community, and was earned by the excellent levels of cooperation between the different village organisations, its clubs and societies.

The fourteenth-century church of St Mary dominates the beautiful little village of Arkesden, only a mile or two to the north. Here there is the added charm of a small stream running through the heart of the village, lined with weeping willows, more ancient thatched dwellings, and crossed at regular intervals by small footbridges with white-painted, picket fence railings. Where the river curves under the trailing willow branches and then passes under a bridge, the road continues up past the green to the church high on the hill.

The road circles back, through Rickling with its huge green, once the site of another long gone Norman castle, and then Quendon, with its Tudor timbered hall set inside a hundred acre park, which was strung out on either side of the main road. You should look for Ugley, a village which belies its name, as it is easy to miss. Ugley has nothing to do with the physical attractions of the village, but is derived from 'Ugga', the name of the Norseman who long ago carved the first inhabited clearing out of the great oak forests which once covered this part of Essex.

However, there is a turn-off signposted to Ugley church, by the Chequers pub, along a one-car lane that takes you through the centre of the village. There is a cluster of three ancient cottages with dark, heavy thatch, and the first discordant note in this charming little tour. On one of the cottage fences was a poster protesting against the planned expansion of Stansted Airport, a reminder that the peace and quiet of this gentle area was under serious threat.

In Ugley there are Bluebell Woods and the beautiful little red-brick tower and red-tiled roofs of St Peter's Church, which make a visit worthwhile. The main body of the church was again faced with large cobbled flints, making patterns of brown, cream and grey in the bright sunlight.

Arkesden, where the stream and the road sweep round below the green and the church.

Turn off through Stansted Mountfitchet, and we have returned to that reconstructed castle, where chickens, sheep and fallow deer roam freely, and everything is presented in a carefully researched picture of life in eleventh-century Britain. Nearby is the House on the Hill Toy Museum, which is a delight for the little ones and for anyone over fifty who wants to wallow in childhood nostalgia.

In the heart of the town there are some fine timbered Tudor buildings, and the lovely red-brick Church of St John is set against a foreground of spring daffodils in the central gardens. To add a final touch of Essex magic there is also a splendid 65ft-high brick tower windmill, built in 1787, making a perfect picture beside a white cottage, with sails spread against a cloud-dappled blue sky.

Finally find your way to Manuden, the heart of this isolated corner of Essex, seemingly dozing in the sun haze of the low green valley of the Stort. It is only a few miles from the starting point at Berden, and almost the completion of this small circular tour.

Manuden is another winding High Street lined on either side with a marvellous array of listed and mediaeval buildings, this time with the river lying just out of sight but parallel to the main road. The flint church tower, topped by a spire, and rising up over the centre of the village and the High Street is again dedicated to St Mary the Virgin.

The origins of the church go back at least as far as the beginning of the twelfth century, although like most mediaeval churches it has been much restored and

Manuden High Street, looking down towards the church.

The Old Inn, the former Cock Inn until 1962, is now a private home.

The Old Maltings.

enlarged over this long period of time. At one stage, in 1863, the original tower became weakened with age and was demolished as unsafe, and virtually the whole building was lengthened and rebuilt.

History here, and for the area as a whole, goes back to long before Domesday, when the village was listed as Magghedana, a name meaning the common valley, and was credited with four manors. However, it would be a mistake to think that all these villages are almost identical, as they each have their own unique charm and character.

The Yew Tree Inn is the only surviving village pub, a sparking white building with an overhung upper storey, named after the wood generally favoured by English archers for the longbows which helped them to win the Battle of Agincourt. Just up the road stands the magnificent ochre-yellow and black-timbered Old Maltings; beside it is a small malt loft with a sharp-angled roof gable that leans out alarmingly over the pavement. The village sign depicts a leatherworker to commemorate another past industry, although generally Manuden was dependent on farming and agriculture for most of its history. Only recently has it become mainly a commuter base, as the need for land workers has been replaced by modern machinery.

There is an abundance of old thatched cottages, but perhaps the most interesting of all is Walnut Tree Cottage which is the first to come into view as you enter Manuden from the road to Bishop's Stortford. Here lived Robert Saville, who robbed and murdered another villager named Thomas Bray in 1789. He was the last man to

Walnut Tree Cottage, believed to be the former home of the last man to be hanged on the Downs.

be hanged on Manuden Downs, facing his mother's cottage. Sleepy Manuden, like all these slumbering villages, was not always and entirely without excitement and incident. In 1431 its vicar, Thomas Bagley, was burned at the stake in Smithfield for heresy. His crime was to support John Wycliffe and the Lollards, who campaigned for religious reform long before the Reformation.

During weekdays these villages are very quiet, almost deserted, and with very little traffic, and yet each one is obviously very much alive with a thriving community spirit. That sleepy, day-time image of time standing still is mainly an illusion.

Almost every one of these small time-mellowed villages is a contender for the title of the jewel of the Essex Highlands. The stream which runs through Arkesden rises at a place called High Wood which at 457ft above sea level is the highest point in Essex, and this little circle of villages is a veritable necklace of beauty spots. It is well worth the trip under the motorway to discover this select and secret corner of the lovely Essex countryside.

CHAPTER EIGHT

THE COLNE VALLEY

The River Colne rises at Ridgewell, not far from the source of the Stour and the Suffolk border, and flows east through the gorgeous Colne valley, through Colchester and out to the sea. On its gently winding way its placid silver waters flow through heritage and history, and some of the most beautiful villages, woodlands and farmlands, in Essex.

The old Roman road from Colchester to Cambridge passed through Ridgewell, where the houses cluster around the spacious green. Here by the river the Romans established one of their military camps. Later when the Normans arrived, in the second great invasion and occupation of our island home, the Norman knight Aubrey de Vere built a massive keep and castle a few miles further down the valley. The great keep still stands at Castle Hedingham, looking across the valley to the twin village of Sible Hedingham on the other side of the river. On this short stretch alone the highlights of over one 1,000 years of English history are already marked.

The Hedinghams are pleasing mixtures of old cottages, houses and inns, each with a mediaeval church, and well worth an exploratory visit in their own right. At Castle Hedingham, in addition to the castle which we have already visited, there is a lovely old timbered moot Hall which is now a restaurant, and the Church of St Nicholas, built by the de Veres, is said to be one of the finest Norman churches in Essex.

Sible Hedingham has almost a mile of main street following the course of the Colne valley and the river. It is here you will find the old water mill that Geoff Wood and his colleagues have been busy restoring to its former glory.

The village is also the birthplace of Sir John Hawkwood, the son of a tanner, a fourteenth-century 'soldier of fortune', and finally a General. Hawkwood served in the French Wars, fighting for Edward III, and eventually formed and led his own White Company, a troop of 3,000 mercenaries. He took his force down into the Italian Peninsular where they fought for various city states, finally becoming the official army of Florence. This remarkable Essex fighting man was buried in Florence

The steeply rising High Street of the ancient market and wool town of Halstead.

Cathedral, although legend says that he was eventually brought back to the church in Sible Hedingham. This seems uncertain, although there was at least a memorial inside the church and its canopy remains.

Here you can also find the Colne Valley Farm Park, with thirty acres of riverside meadows to explore, and the head of the restored section of the Colne Valley Steam Railway.

The Colne Valley & Halstead Railway came through Sible Hedingham in 1861, and stayed until Dr Beeching made it all redundant in the 1950s. Some ten years later, two railway enthusiasts took an evening stroll along a mile-long section of the old track bed that followed close to the course of the river, and decided there and then to recreate the whole thing. Their passion helped to fire a whole team of volunteers and the old Sible & Castle Hedingham railway station was dismantled brick by brick and rebuilt in its present location. The track way was cleared of undergrowth and new tracks laid, and in August of 1973 the first locomotive reappeared, brought in on a low loader by road, but blowing a head of steam and a triumphant whistle to announce its proud arrival.

Three more locomotives soon followed, two 200ft platforms were built, and the necessary signal boxes and passenger carriages arrived. A restaurant car became a permanent restaurant. The site continues to acquire rolling stock and exhibits, and today the Colne Valley Railway is a working steam railway station, running regular passenger trips up and down a mile of restored track beside the river. The train doesn't actually

Townford Mill, built by the Courtauld Family, is now an Antiques Centre.

go anywhere, but it's a popular family day out. Children love it, and most adults seem equally pleased with this particular slice of railway nostalgia. This 'just-for-fun' line actually carries as many passengers per year as the real railway did in its heyday.

Continue down the valley and you will come to the ancient wool town of Halstead. Many of the smart shops along the steep High Street were once the homes of the wealthy traders and merchants who prospered from the wool and silk weaving industries that dominated the town from the fifteenth century onwards. The Courtauld family settled here in the 1820s and were the mainstay of Halstead's business life for the next 100 years. They built the beautiful white, weather-board Townford Mill, now flourishing again as an antiques centre, which still spans the river in the heart of the town.

At the top of the High Street stands the prominent Jubilee Fountain and crowning the hill looking down over all it surveys is the solid square flint tower of fourteenth-century St Andrew's Church. At the bottom of the hill is another fourteenth-century building, the lovely old timber-framed Bull Hotel.

The river flows on, through rich pasture and arable farmland, and winds its way through villages which all take its name, Colne Engaine, Earl's Colne, White Colne, and Wake's Colne. Earl's Colne is the largest of the four, named after Alberic de Vere, the Earl of Oxford, who received the village and the whole estate of its former Saxon overlord as a gift from William the Conqueror. The de Vere coat of arms is carved in stone on the splendid red-brick tower of the Church of St Andrew.

The towering Victorian archways of Chappel Viaduct.

At Wake's Colne, the road and the river pass under one of the thirty-two towering Victorian brick arches of the Chappel Viaduct, which march across the entire width of the valley. The whole span is a stupendous 1,066ft long. Here there is more railway nostalgia at the East Anglian Railway Museum at Chappel Station. The original station with its booking hall and platforms, signal boxes, workshops and good yards, have all been lovingly restored and maintained. Trains still pass through, and the whole place is a treasure trove of steam age memorabilia.

While at Chappel, don't miss one of the smallest, but prettiest little churches along the whole valley, the little red-roofed church of St Barnabas, with its elegant white boarded belfry and spire.

The river flows on, through the heart of Colchester, 'the oldest recorded town in Britain'; the quote is mandatory, as is a mention of the Roman walls, the Norman castle, and the mediaeval ruins of St Botolph's Priory. Here again, almost all of English history is encapsulated in one small area. A major battle of the English Civil War was also fought out here, when Royalist forces held the town for their king against an eleven-week siege by Cromwell's Roundheads. Finally the old Roman walls were breached, the town fell, and the Royalist leaders were executed by being shot in front of the castle, where a simple memorial stone now stands.

A walk around the walls is still one of the best ways to explore Colchester. They were built after the Iceni-Queen Boudicca besieged, destroyed and burned the town in AD 60, and have surrounded the re-built town centre for almost 2,000 years.

The Roman walls at Colchester.

About a mile and half of crumbling ruins still remain in sections along Balkerne Hill, Priory Street, and flanking two sides of Castle Park, perhaps half of the original circumference. They can also be found underground in the cellars along Sir Isaac's Walk. The Lemon Tree, fronting St John's Street, even has a cellar restaurant that incorporates a Roman archway.

A good place to start is the Balkerne Gate beside the Hole in the Wall pub. As you turn south and then east you can dip in and out of the town centre to visit a series of lovely old churches, the priory ruins, and then turn north to pass the castle. A short diversion will take you down East Hill to find the Siege House, a battle-scarred old black and white timbered building famous for the musket damage left over from the Civil War.

Back up East Hill and into the High Street takes you to the splendid red-brick and white stone Town Hall, a richly columned and sculpted Italian-style masterpiece. It stands on the site of the old Moot Hall that served Colchester as an administrative centre for 700 years before being pulled down in 1843. A second town hall was built which lasted for only fifty years before it too was outgrown by the town and its needs, and so at the turn of the century the present Town Hall was constructed. Inside there are council chambers, offices and law courts, and a splendidly ornate assembly room which is still called the Moot Hall. In niches on the outside walls are a host of statues representing the history of the borough, including Boudicca, King Edward the Elder, and Eudo Dapifer, who built the castle. High above the clock tower is a bronze statue of Helena, Roman goddess and mother of the Emperor Constantine, and the patron saint of Colchester.

Off to your right now is the Old Dutch Quarter that still has the timber-framed homes of the Flemish weavers who settled there in the fifteenth century. They fled from religious persecution in their own country, but the skills they brought with them injected a new prosperity to the flagging weaving industry, and helped to make Colchester into another thriving wool centre.

Finally one must mention Jumbo, the massive square brick water tower that dominates the skyline in tandem with the much more elegant Town Hall tower. An eyesore to some, another triumph of Victorian architecture to others, Jumbo insists on not being ignored. The tower was recently sold for £300,000 and plans have been revealed to convert the interior into flats and a restaurant. Whatever the result, Jumbo as a recognisable landmark will hopefully remain.

The river flows past the park, loops around the town and continues east. It passes the old Hythe Quay, a place busy through past centuries with Roman galleys, mediaeval tall ships, and then the old Thames barges, all loading and unloading a variety of passengers and trade goods. All of that is gone now, lost in the past with the fading footfalls of the dead Roman soldier who is supposed to have once haunted the crumbling walls.

Leaving Colchester, the river flows to the south of Wivenhoe Park and the tall, modern tower blocks of Essex University, and down to Rowbridge and Wivenhoe. Here was the real port of Colchester. Most of the cargoes were later discharged here because Rowbridge was the highest point where the bigger boats could turn round.

The Victorian tower of the Town Hall dominates Colchester High Street.

Now, due to the flood barrier built downstream, Wivenhoe has also lost most of its sea-borne trade. Modern housing estates are built over the sites of the old quays, but the town itself is still very much a one-way street which curves past the church and dead-ends on what must be one of the most attractive waterfronts in the county.

They began building ships here in the fifteenth century, and there are still men who can remember when Wivenhoe was a busy port and fishing village with boatyards on both sides of the quay. Fishing in the winter and yacht-crewing in the summer was the traditional seasonal pattern of work, with all-year-round commercial traffic having right of way in the middle of the river. Smuggling was not unknown, and there were many houses with a secret cubby-hole where you could hide away the odd barrel of rum.

Later, yacht-building and yacht racing became the order of the day, and Wivenhoe is still a popular port of call with pleasure sailors. On a high summer day the waterfront is the perfect place to sit outside the Rose and Crown with a pint of ale and simply watch the boats go by.

The river widens now as it flows on to Brightlingsea, another old port with a long history, which is now past its commercial and shipbuilding prime. The Romans built a fort here as part of their defences for Colchester, and later, in the Middle Ages, it became one of the Cinque Ports of England, granted extensive tax free privileges of trade in return for an agreement to provide ships of war for the king when needed. To quote just two examples, in 1347 Brightlingsea provided ships and men for Edward III's siege of Calais, and again for Sir Francis Drake's attack on Lisbon in 1589.

Once the great days of its maritime age had passed, Brightlingsea still thrived as a fishing port, with a lively trade in sprats and oysters. In the 1930s there was a large fishing fleet of Colchester smacks, and huge quantities of sprats were landed at Brightlingsea. The glistening, sun-kissed creeks and mudflats around the estuary also provided perfect conditions for shellfish, and oysters have been a popular sea food since Roman times. In Colchester they still hold an annual oyster feast every year in the Moot Hall of the Town hall.

After the Second World War, Brightlingsea became, like Wivenhoe, a centre for yacht-building and yacht racing. The lovely old, double gabled, black and white Customs House still stands above the concrete hard that slopes down into the river, but now it shares the small waterfront with the Colne Yacht Club.

The soaring tower of All Saints' Church stands on a hilltop on an approach road overlooking the town. It provides a landmark that can be seen for many miles by both land and sea. It is truly a sailor's church, for inside there are more than 200 tile tablets to commemorate the names of Brightlingsea sailors who have lost their lives to the hungry sea.

The Colne finally flows into the North Sea at Point Clear, just below Brightlingsea. On the way the towns and villages along its banks have a multitude of tales to tell, of

Brightlingsea, with the old Customs House and the Yacht Club.

Romans and Saxons, of rampaging Vikings and invading Norman knights, of farmers and wool merchants, fishermen and smugglers. It is a river with an on-going history, sparkling with memories.

CHAPTER NINE

MARITIME WIVENHOE

We are not yet ready to leave the River Colne and its maritime history. The Romans had a taste for its oysters and fed them to their armies, and later cheap and plentiful oysters fed the poor of London. Fishing was always a livelihood for those who lived here, and shipbuilding went back to the sixteenth century. The small freighters bringing in timber and coal, and taking out flour and sand; the streams of barges ploughing up to Colchester, and fleets of fishing smacks heading out to reap up the sprat harvest in the open sea are still part of some living memories.

Maritime Wivenhoe has seen it all come and go and has always been a central part of the river traffic. In the last chapter we passed it by too quickly, and with old street names like Smugglers Cottages and Captain's Row it is worth a closer look. The bigger ships that couldn't get up to Colchester discharged their cargoes here. Mike Downes can recall pushing himself off the steel hull of a coaster, and other yacht sailors remember being frequently run aground into the mud on either side to give the right of way to the larger ships in mid-river.

The Nottage Maritime Institute on Wivenhoe Quay.

Wivenhoe waterfront.

The quays of this little port town were always busy. Sprats were the poor man's sardine, and those that were too large or too small to go into the tins were given away, which meant that in season the smell of frying sprats gave the town its own distinct flavour and aroma. If the fishing was too good, and there was a glut of sprats, they would be spread on the surrounding fields as manure.

Things have changed of course – ships got larger, and the continual dredging of the river became too costly. When the flood barrier was built down river from Wivenhoe most of the commercial traffic on the Colne came to an end. The barges disappeared, the larger ships went elsewhere, a handful of fishing craft remain, and the great bulk of the river traffic now is in yachts and pleasure craft.

Smart, modern new housing now replaces much of the old waterfronts, but part of the old quay at Wivenhoe still remains. Boats still moor here, in front of the Rose and Crown, and the old sailing loft that is now the Nottage Maritime Institute. It all has a timeless feel and flavour, despite the changes, and it is here that the spirit of maritime Wivenhoe is still nourished and maintained. The story of the Nottage is the story of Wivenhoe and the Colne as one era ended and another began.

The Nottage has seen its centenary. It was founded just over 100 years ago by Captain Charles George Nottage, who left the sum of £3,000 in his will for that purpose. A considerable sum for the time.

Captain Nottage (the rank was military, although he did skipper his own yachts) was born in 1852. The family wealth came from his father, who founded the London

1. Southend's flower gardens are among its main attractions.

2. At night the bright and vivacious side of Southend comes buoyantly alive.

3. The Mill Pool at Flatford.

4. Harwich Quay is a good place to watch the big ships go by.

5. A glade in Epping Forest, once the haunt of highwaymen and now a playground for cyclists and walkers.

6. A narrow boat approaches the lock gates at Harlow Mill.

7. The tower keep at Hedingham Castle, one of the best preserved Norman remains in Europe.

8. Colchester Castle is built on the foundation platform of the Roman temple to Claudius.

9. At Colchester, these ruined arches and columns are all that remain of St Botolph's Priory.

10. Ancient walls and a monumental towered gateway screen the remaining buildings of St Osyth's Priory from public view.

11. Finchingfield, a thatched cottage and a windmill on the hill, the essence of rural Essex.

12. Thaxted windmill and the soaring spire of St John's Church.

13. The magic of Manuden: thatched cottages and the spire of the village church.

14. The beauty of Ugley is summed up by the red-tiled roofs and sun-dappled flint cobbles of St Peter's.

15. The peaceful Colne wends its way through the heart of Halstead.

16. Railway nostalgia abounds at the East Anglian Railway Museum at Chappel Station.

17. Picturesque Wivenhoe, the old waterfront from the river.

18. Modern housing now stands on some of the old quays.

19. Maldon waterfront, maritime Essex at its best.

20. Inside St Mary's Church, this glorious stained-glass window shows the souls of Brynoth and his men ascending to heaven.

21. Andrew Edwards and Richard Haward
sorting through the catch.

22. One of Heather Haward's gourmet sea
food platters.

23. Great Dunmow Town Hall.

24. Great Dunmow, Doctor's Pond and Jubilee railings.

25. At Battlesbridge, this lovely old mill is now an antiques centre.

26. The River Crouch at Burnham.

27. The Church of St George with its charming lych gate.

28. One of the prettiest churches in the Colne Valley, St Barnabas at Chappel.

29. The manicured lawns and elegant flower beds of Audley End.

30. The Old Sun Inn at Saffron Walden, which is decorated with some of the best known pargeting work in the whole of England.

31. The Cavaliers charge into action against Cromwell's cavalry at the Battle of Naseby.

32. Pikemen clash as The Battle of Naseby is re-enacted at Audley End.

Small boats still line Wivenhoe Quay.

The Colne from the balcony of the Nottage Institute, once the superstructures of ships sailed past, but today it is mainly yachts.

Stereoscopic & Photographic Company in 1856. The company manufactured the first cameras, which were immediately popular with the very rich, and Nottage senior was undoubtedly a very gifted entrepreneur. He had astute business and social skills and was later made Lord Mayor of London.

Charles George Nottage was a keen sportsman and world traveller, and eventually took an interest in yachting and yacht racing. He made three world tours, walked through the interiors of Japan and Central Russia, and spent a long period in the South Seas. He was elected a Fellow of the Royal Geographical Society in 1880, but despite his global wandering, it seems that his heart was always with the River Colne.

Yacht-building flourished on the Colne because the boatyards here built the fastest vessels. Smuggling had always been a popular supplement to fishing, especially prior to the Napoleonic wars with France, which put the trade into a temporary decline. However, most Wivenhoe houses in the nineteenth century were still built with a secret cubby-hole to hide the odd brandy cask, or barrel of rum, and Wivenhoe built both the swift vessels the smugglers needed, and the fast cutters with which the revenue men tried hard to catch them.

Finally, as the traditional occupations of smuggling and fishing began to fade away, so yacht owning and racing became fashionable. It seems to have started with groups of young lords and ladies amusing themselves with mock battles in which they played with miniature warships as they tried to cut each others' rigging. The competitive spirit of these games developed into yacht racing, and Wivenhoe and the Colne, where the revenue men and the smugglers had always striven to out-run and pursue each other, was the obvious place to find the skills to build world-class racers.

It was also the place to find the sailors to crew them. Most Colne residents were fishermen in the winter and yacht crewmen in the summer. Yacht crewing had definite advantages – a regular wage, not being dependent on the weather and the catch, a chance to visit the pleasure ports of the Mediterranean, and in the racing season a possible share in the prize money. A few fishermen might have preferred their independence, but most of them jumped at the new opportunities, and competition for places on the shiny new yachts was fierce.

Captain Charles Nottage came to know many of these men as he worked and sailed beside them. They had only the fishing and sailing skills that their fathers had handed down to them, with little or no chance for further advancement. Charles Nottage wanted to change all that, to give them some scope at self-improvement, and better opportunities for the future. So the idea of the Nottage Institute was born; a free education for those who wanted to become more proficient in the arts of navigation and sailing.

Sadly his health deteriorated, and he died in 1895 while still only forty-two years old. But his will had provided for the foundation of the Nottage Institute. Today the Nottage is run by a large group of its trustees, its management committee,

The institute's walls are crowded with memorabilia, and models of the fishing craft that once plied the Colne.

and tutors, all of them volunteers who give freely of their time.

The upper floor of the converted sail-maker's loft, where once sails were stretched out for repairs, is now divided into a large lecture room with models, old photographs and other memorabilia lining the walls, and a library that now houses one of the largest collections of maritime books and maps in Essex. In the library I met and talked with Chairman Dan Chapman, Vice Chairman Iain Ward, Warden Mike Downes, and Austin Baines, the Chairman of the Artifacts Sub-Committee. Dan explains:

For about the first sixty years tuition was provided free of charge. We had lads coming from as far away as West Mersea to learn about navigation and related subjects, all at the Nottage's expense, including their travelling expenses. But then, about thirty years ago, there was a crisis because funds were dropping and our running expenses were exceeding our income. A second branch of the Nottage had been opened up at Cowes on the Isle of Wight, but that had to go, and even here we were in difficulty.

Things were changing, of course, and the need for free tuition that Captain Nottage had envisioned for ordinary seamen was drying up. The old sail and barge traffic was dying out, and the Nottage also went into decline. That was when it was decided to bring in tuition for boat and yacht owners, rather than for crewmen, and to charge them and turn it into a business.

Iain Ward (left), and Mike Downes, demonstrate the art of boat-building.

Iain added:

> Up until the war there was always a job for local men on the yachts.But after the war when people began to get back into sailing again it became much more a picture of amateurs doing their own thing.The commercial sailing was drying up, and it was all leisure sailing.

Dan continues:

> There has been this changeover. Although it has been gradual and the process is still continuing. So we are now providing help and education to yacht owners rather than crewmen. We are now running fifteen different courses in various stages of navigation and seamanship, radio operating, engine maintenance, boat construction, sail-trimming and rig-tuning, and traditional boating skills.
>
> We only do theory courses here, but these give every student the foundation and background they need to go on to an authorized school to get their ticket. We can't provide free classes any more, but we are non-profit-making, and we are all volunteers. We do teach people to sail properly and we are able to give very good value for money.

Mike interjected:

> And the difference it makes to have a boat rigged properly is unbelievable. I always point out to people that they wouldn't drive their car without the wheels being properly

balanced and the engine timing right, so why struggle to sail a boat that isn't properly rigged and trimmed?

Maintaining the old crafts and skills is another key feature here, and we moved below to where up to a dozen wooden boats were in various stages of construction. Dan explains:

Our boat-building classes are very popular. Students build their own boats here, and take them away and sail them when they are finished. It can take up to 400 hours to build a boat, and there is always a waiting list of people wanting to get on the course. In between classes students are free to come in and work on their boat at any time that the institute is open. The courses perpetuate the traditional skills of boat-building, and they also provide us with an effective display of the various construction stages that always seem to interest our visitors.

The Institute is, of course, also a maritime museum, and another of its purposes is to keep alive the spirit of maritime Wivenhoe through the preservation of records, archives and artefacts which relate to the fascinating history of the town and the river.

Finally, the Nottage also runs a small ferry over to Rowhedge in the summer season and at weekends. A mile up river on the opposite bank, Rowhedge is the smaller, slightly less fashionable sister village to Wivenhoe. Here, too, most of the old quays have disappeared under new developments. Douglas Meyers, the ferryman, was another volunteer giving freely and cheerfully of his time. He took me up and down the river to get my photographs. It was a splendid October morning with the bright sunlight dancing on the steel-blue waters, but sadly there was neither a fisherman nor a smuggler in sight.

The one small quay that remains at Wivenhoe still has all the charm of the old port, with boats and masts still lining its moorings. The twelfth-century church tower of St Mary's rises square and solid behind the old black clapboard buildings, cottages in pastel pink, and the bright yellow of the Rose and Crown. Set square in the centre of the quay, is the solid red-brick of the Nottage Maritime Institute, with its dark blue balcony and blue-painted doors.

Here the essence of maritime Essex is kept alive in a permanent exhibition of Wivenhoes' nautical history. From its windows you could once watch the superstructure of large coastal ships, or the white sails of the big yachts go sailing by. Today it is mostly memories and small pleasure boats that hover around the last stretch of quayside.

CHAPTER TEN

BLACKWATER BYWAYS

Finchingfield is the quintessential Essex village, complete with a large expanse of village green, a duck pond, a neatly humped red-brick bridge, a white boarded windmill, thatched cottages, and a 450-year-old guildhall half way up the hill, standing at the entrance to the churchyard under the comforting shade of a fourteenth-century church tower. In 1951, when the Festival of Britain Committee decided to select and promote a handful of the prettiest villages in England, Finchingfield was one of their obvious choices.

Finchingfield, a classic Essex village.

This is one of the loveliest corners of the county and the little stream that flows through the centre of the village runs into the gentle river Pant. The Pant rises just to the west of Radwinter, and passes between Great and Little Sampford, three more equally idyllic little villages, before flowing on through Shalford to the larger town of Braintree. Here it becomes the Blackwater and continues on to the sea.

Braintree is one of those ancient market towns which flourished comfortably with the wool trade in the Middle Ages. Before that it was a Saxon town and before that a Roman town. Its market charter was granted in 1199 and there are still twice-weekly markets when the Great Square at the top of the High Street and the Market Square beyond are filled with colourful stalls and crowded with shoppers. It is all overlooked by the elegant white clock tower above the red-brick Georgian Town Hall.

The clock tower is topped by the golden figure of a child looking into a mirror. It is allegorical and represents the Courtauld family motto: 'Hold to the Truth.' Below the clock, on the front face, is the red and gold coat of arms of the urban district, which also incorporates the Courtauld coat of arms. The Courtaulds were the dominant force

in the silk industry which replaced the wool trade at the turn of the nineteenth century, and continued to promote the general prosperity of the town. The Town Hall was just one of the family gifts to the town, which also included the hospital and the circular fountain with the statue of a young man arising from a shell, which stands in front of St Michael's Church with its distinctive shingle spire.

The River Brain curls through the southern half of Braintree, while Bocking End, where most of the oldest town buildings are

Braintree market, overlooked by the elegant white clock tower above the Georgian Town Hall.

located, leads roughly north to the bridge where the Pant becomes the Blackwater. The two rivers, so essential to the mediaeval wool trade, do not actually join until they reach Witham.

On the way, the Blackwater wriggles lazily down to Coggeshall, another once important wool town. Here there are more ancient, meandering streets, lined with equally ancient buildings, often timbered with overhanging upper stories, all radiating out from the market square, and overlooked by the tall, blue hexagonal clock tower erected to commemorate Queen Victoria's Jubilee. One of the old village wool halls has survived and is now the White Hart Hotel.

They are all eclipsed by Paycocke's House, which tends to draw the attention of visitors away from all the rest that Coggeshall has to offer. This magnificent building stands on West Street. The close vertical timbers are spaced out with herringbone bricks, with the overhanging eaves, the doorposts and window frames, all lavishly carved with a variety of figures and motifs. It epitomises all the pomp and pride of a wealthy mediaeval wool merchant.

Paycocke's House at Coggeshall.

Coggeshall is also the site of a Cistercian abbey, founded by King Stephen in 1140. The monks are said to have introduced brick-making to the country as a whole, and sheep farming to the area in particular. The abbey disappeared after the Dissolution; the site is occupied by a farm built partly from its ruins, and all that remains now is the Grange Barn, their vast, timber-built storehouse, which is one of the oldest in Europe.

However, if you have an interest in spectacular mediaeval barns, then Cressing Temple is only a few miles away. Here there are two of them, built by the Knights Templar in the thirteenth century to store the vast harvests from their farm holdings in the area. The Knights were sworn to protect pilgrims on the way to Jerusalem, and despite their monastic vows of poverty, chastity and obedience, they grew to be a very rich and powerful international order. In fact they built up too much wealth and power, which ultimately contributed to their downfall. They became a rival to Popes and kings and had to be suppressed.

Witham, where the Brain eventually feeds into the Blackwater, was once owned by the Knights Templar. The old Roman road to Colchester crossed the river here, but even before there were roads, any meeting point of natural waterways inevitably developed into a trading centre. When the Knights arrived on the mediaeval scene they were keen to develop this potential. They established Witham's first market.

The River Blackwater, fed and strengthened by all those subsidiary waters, flows on to Maldon and the wide Blackwater Estuary that opens out to the sea. Maldon is maritime Essex at its best, an important Saxon fishing port, which still retains much of the flavour of its ancient heritage. The estuary with its surrounding maze of creeks and mudflats has always been rich in fish and shellfish, a focus for sea-borne trade, coastal and to the continent, and a natural route for invasion.

The white, wooden steeple above the stone tower of St Mary's dominates the skyline of the town above Hythe Quay. This well-known 'Mariner's Beacon' welcomes yacht and barge skippers as they sail up the last few twists and turns of the river. The quay itself

Pride of the past: the old Thames barges still moor at Maldon.

is still a haven for the tall masts of a handful of the lovely old Thames barges that still survive from the eighteenth century, and for a multitude of more modern craft.

Inside the church there is a beautiful blue, gold and purple stained-glass window to commemorate the Battle of Maldon which took place in 991. A Viking fleet had sacked Ipswich to the north, and then sailed up the Blackwater to make their base camp on Northey Island which sits in the mouth of the estuary opposite the town. Bryhtnoth, the local Saxon Earl, had gathered the men of Essex to fight the Danes, but he made one fatal mistake. His sense of honour and English fair play caused him to let the Viking army cross the tidal causeway and form up their battle lines on the mainland before he attacked. It cost him his life and the battle. Now, in the glory of stained glass inside the church, the souls of Brythnoth and his men are seen floating up from their graves to take their place in heaven.

At the top of the High Street, past the old Moot Hall half way up on the right, stands the splendid thirteenth-century, flint and stone church of All Saints with its unique triangular tower. Here there is another stained-glass window which is well worth seeking out. This is the Washington window, given by the citizens of Maldon Massachusetts, a town founded in the USA by Essex immigrants over 300 years ago. The window is in memory of George Washington's great grandfather, who is buried in the churchyard here. In scenes of glorious coloured glass, Columbus lands in America, the Pilgrim Fathers arrive, and George Washington signs the Declaration of Independence.

In its barge traffic heyday, 2,000 of the old sailing barges, out of the 5,000 or so that plied the eastern coastline, are said to have operated out of Maldon. Their gross tonnage was usually in excess of 100 tons, and they carried anything from mud to grain. The famous Maldon Stackie could, and did, carry a haystack. Their flat bottom design made them ideal for shallow coastal waters, rivers and inlets, and the masts with the great rust-red sails could be lowered to enable them to pass under bridges. Their trading days are gone, but those that survive are lovingly maintained, to be used for holiday and charter cruises, and for taking part in all the annual sailing barge matches along the Blackwater and other major East Coast rivers, to remember the days when they raced in earnest to pursue the cargoes that were the life blood of their existence.

Each race lasts over one day, with the course planned at the last minute and dependent on the winds, tides and weather forecast for the day. Around a score or more of barges will sail out of the Blackwater into the North Sea, circle round the course and race back again for the finish line in a set time limit.

I watched one race finish from the promenade along the river as the tall masts slowly hove in to view, most with sails furled but one with a magnificent spread of full red sails, as they zigzagged with infinite grace and drifting laziness up the invisible stretches of the Blackwater. The tops of the masts moved left to right, then right to left, and then left to right again, each sweep showing them larger and more distinct across the green banks and trees hiding the lower reaches of the river. Then at last they reappeared in their full size and glory to bear down the last curve toward the Hythe Quay.

They were under motor power for the last lap, for the tide and the river were still low, but in their heyday, before there were engines, they would have had to wait for high tide to give them more room to manoeuvre under sail. What a splendid sight they would have all made then. One by one they tied up at the quay, a growing forest of soaring masts with lashed red sails, the black, red and gold hulls moored side-by-side and pushing ever further out into mid-stream.

On the northern shore of the estuary are the villages of Goldhanger and Tollesbury. At Goldhanger, the wide tidal waters have receded from the head of the creek, where at one time the resident fishing smacks would unload their catch, but at Tollesbury there is now a large yacht marina. Here a row of tall, white-boarded sail-makers' lofts have been smartly restored, retaining some of the impact it would have had as a purely fishing community a century ago. In the parish church, the lectern is carved with a plough and a sailing ship, the twin symbols of Tollesbury's heritage.

On the southern shore of the estuary is the widespread community of Mayland, another large sailing centre where, during the Second World War, Cardnell's boatyard turned out motor torpedo boats for the Navy. At Bradwell, where the Blackwater finally turns out into the North Sea the past and the present meet. Here on isolated Sale Point, alone against the marsh and the sea, sits the tiny chapel of St Peter's On the Wall.

This tiny Saxon chapel is all that is left of a monastery built on the site of the old Roman fort of Othona, one of the chain of Roman-built fortifications, used to protect the wild Essex coast. The sea has wiped away most traces of the old fort, although the inner wall forms part of the foundation of the later chapel. From here, in the seventh century a monk from Lindisfarne, later to become St Cedd, set about the task of converting the people of Essex to Christianity.

Not far away, in complete contrast, is Bradwell power station, one of the first nuclear power stations to be built in England. Opened in 1962, it generated electricity for forty years until 2002. Its time has now also passed and it too has become obsolete, the massive square blocks presiding silently over their own ghosts, as well as those of the ancient Romans and Saxons who once passed by.

Opposite Bradwell is Mersea Island, more marsh and creeks and a multitude of pleasure boats, and, of course, oysters. The oysters are still dredged up from the deep mid-river channels, to be re-laid and fattened up in the warm, shallow waters of the muddy inlets.

The rivers that feed the Blackwater have travelled from the country heart of Essex, through hundreds of years of history and heritage to the sea.

The restored sail-makers' lofts at Tollesbury.

Mersea Island, a vista of marsh and river, small creeks and an endless variety of small boats.

CHAPTER ELEVEN

FEASTING ON OYSTERS

We cannot leave the estuaries of the Blackwater and the Colne without taking a closer look at what was once their major industry, the oyster fisheries. Oyster harvesting still goes on, and on the last Friday in every October the Lord Mayor of Colchester and around 300 invited guests will still sit down to enjoy the traditional annual Colchester Oyster Feast. After the Mayor's Chaplain has said grace, they will probably begin again with Pyefleet Native Oysters served with brown bread and butter and a glass of Guinness. To follow will be a magnificent meal with an impressive wine and champagne accompaniment, speeches, and toasts, a splendid programme of music, and, of course, the national anthem.

The setting for this splendid corporation feast is the vast and richly decorated Moot Hall, its high, arched roof hung with chandeliers and supported by rows of paired Greek columns, separated by high, stained-glass windows depicting a summary history of the borough. The original Moot Hall was a twelfth-century mediaeval meeting hall, Moot being the Anglo-Saxon word for a meeting, which served as Colchester's main administrative and judicial building for nearly 700 years. The present Moot Hall is the main assembly room inside the present Town Hall, which was built in Victorian times on the same spot.

Native oysters were being harvested in the tidal estuaries around Mersea Island and the mouth of the Colne even before the Romans discovered them and found them to their liking, so oyster feasting is nothing new. The annual Colchester Oyster Feast also goes back so far that no one actually knows when or why it originated. In the time of Charles II it was already well established and always took place on the eve of St Dennis Day, the first day of the St Dennis Fair. In the day-to-day slog of the Middle Ages, there were probably few scholars around to worry about the whys and wherefores and dates of origins. If a feast or a fair came along you took time off and enjoyed it, and that still seems a fair enough philosophy even for today.

The start of the oyster fishery season will have been duly marked at the end of August by another annual tradition, a regular Gin and Gingerbread Ceremony. This one takes place afloat in the Pyefleet Channel off East Mersea with the Mayor reading an ancient proclamation to declare the season open before the first dredge of the season is made. It's all in full regalia, of course, and the mandatory toast to the Queen is made, followed by a message sent to Her Majesty to inform her that the custom has been kept.

The oystermen also have their own start to the season in the form of an oyster dredging match. Many of the old fishing smacks which used to work under sail are still afloat, although they are now sailed for pleasure. Up to a dozen of them will now come together in September just to keep alive the spirit of those old sail fishing days. The boats have a set time and place to dredge and then race back for the weigh-in. There are prizes for the best time, the best weight, and most professional handling of the boat.

To find out more about the background to the oyster fisheries and the real job of cultivating and harvesting these popular delicacies, I went down to West Mersea and talked to Richard Haward. Richard owns his own 22ft skiff and his own oyster layings, while his wife Heather owns the well-known Company Shed, so it would have been difficult to find a couple who knew more about all the various aspects of the industry. Richard explained::

My family have been in oyster fishing for 200 years. So with one of my sons now giving it a go that makes eight generations of Hawards who must have oyster fishing in their blood.

There have been many ups and downs in all that time. In the nineteenth century they practically fed the poor of London on oysters, and the indentured London apprentices eventually rebelled and insisted that they should not be fed oysters more than twice a week. But there have also been times when oysters have been very, very scarce. You might get a period of several bad years, and then perhaps a prolific year that will sustain commercial fishing for several more years, and that has been the pattern for a long time.

The slumps might be due to over-fishing, or pollution, or a combination of natural circumstances. If the spawning conditions are not right, say the water temperatures are not warm enough, or the food supply is insufficient, then things just don't happen. The big freeze of 1963 almost wiped out the river. Then, in the 1980s, we had a problem with bonamia ostreae, which was an oyster disease, and also with TBT, a very toxic anti-fouling product that was sold to keep the bottoms of boats clean. It did do a marvellous job on the boats, but it also did a not-so-marvellous job on the marine environment. It stopped the native oysters spawning and the Pacific Gigas oysters we had imported to increase stock just wouldn't grow. The stuff was eventually banned, but it was four or five years before the native oysters started to spawn again.

In 1984 a small group of us took over the majority shareholding of the Tollesbury and Mersea Native Oyster Fishery Company. There are free fishing areas on the river, but the company holds a Several Fishery Order, which is like a government lease, on the main part of the river. At the time things were not looking good, but we thought there could be a future, so we started to work on cleaning the seabed.

It was a slow job, because these things don't happen overnight. We used a farmer's harrow to drag along the bottom and clear away all the weed and sediment, because oysters need a clean bottom to settle. They have to cling to a rock or a piece of shell, or something solid. Often they cling to each other, and when we harvest them we may have to carefully separate several small ones from one large one, and then throw the small ones back.

For the first few years we only did the cleaning. We didn't want to harvest any until we had built the stocks back up. Then we started on a little dredging just to pay for the cleaning operation. Now we're harvesting a few each year, but still leaving many more there to spawn and increase the stock.

'It's not just a fishing operation,' he concluded seriously. 'It's an on-going conservation and cultivation programme. There is a lot more involved than most people realise.'

To complete my education Richard took me out into the river mouth to the oyster dredger *Verley Native,* where Skipper William Baker and his crewman Andrew Edwards welcomed me on board. The *Verley Native* was a compact boat, ideal for working the sea, the river, and the creeks that split the surrounding marshland. At 26ft with a Cygnus fibreglass hull and a 120hp diesel engine, she had a working table at the

Left: Skipper William Baker mans the winches.

Below: The *Verley Native* dredging for oysters.

stern and a solid metal frame to support the winch cables that pulled up the triangular dredging frames with their steel ringed nets.

Each haul was emptied on to the working table and quickly sorted. The large oysters went into buckets and trays, the smaller oysters, stones and other debris were then pushed back over the stern. It was a perfectly calm day and the winches whirred as the two dredge nets dipped in and out of the sea with alternating regularity. Starfish were tossed into a corner of the deck and left to expire. Despite their pretty and harmless appearance, starfish are in fact a predatory pest that will wrap themselves around an oyster shell and suck the goodness out of it.

William and Andrew had been working since 6 a.m., and by 3 p.m. they had caught their quota for the day. At that point they ceased dredging and left the main river to cruise up into one of the creeks where William had his layings. We sailed up an avenue of clear water between long lines of moored pleasure boats.

There seemed to be thousands of pleasure craft dotting these waters, but, as Andrew informed me, only about two dozen are working boats, and now only four of those are engaged in the oyster industry.

Finally the oysters were weighed, before being dropped back over the side in flat trays. Oysters would spawn in the main river, William explained, and they could be sold straight from the main river, but they would be poor oysters. However, by relaying them in the quieter creeks, where the water temperature and the feeding conditions were at

Left: Hauling up another full dredge net of oysters.

Below: Emptying the dredge net on to the working table at the stern of the boat.

The premier place for sea food in Essex, The Company Shed.

Richard and Heather Haward at the sea food counter inside The Company Shed.

the optimum, the oysters would fatten into the juicy, succulent delicacy that the true connoisseurs would expect. It was also easier to market them from the beds, where the quantity as well as the quality could be guaranteed.

After seeing for myself how the oysters were fished and brought home, it was time to return to shore to see how they were prepared and sold. Rick Stein's popular *Food Heroes* programme on television was based on the principle of, 'Seeking out people to whom the flavour of food was more important than its profit.' So it must have been inevitable that the gastronomic trail would lead him down into Essex and West Mersea, to sample England's most succulent oysters, and one of Heather Haward's superb sea food platters at the renowned Company Shed.

The trail, of course, was blazed 2,000 years ago by the Romans, who first found Essex oysters to their liking and built the Strood, the causeway that links Mersea Island to the mainland. Cockles and mussels are found here too, and the sea off the mouths of the Colne and the Blackwater provide the lobsters, crabs, shrimp, and all the rich variety of fish which help to make up those huge platters.

Heather admitted that they do buy in Salmon from outside. 'Everything else is brought in by fishing boats that fish out of West Mersea. People sometimes ask for a particular fish, and I have to say sorry, but at the moment they're not catching any. We're here to sell West Mersea fish, fresh as it comes in from the sea,' Heather explained.

We talked as we sat at one of the tables in The Company Shed, still too early for customers to be eating, although there was a regular stream at the counter buying wet fish to take home. Outside the sea was liberally strewn with a multitude of small pleasure craft that lay sparkling silver beyond a narrow strip of mudflats and boatyards. On the harbour by the Hard where the fishing boats were moored a scattering of artists sat or stood at their easels, all busily capturing different aspects of the idyllic scene in oils or watercolours.

The Company Shed was just that – an old oyster-purifying shed that Heather and Richard had purchased eighteen years before with the idea that it would be a good place from which to sell wet fish. It was never intended to be a restaurant, and Heather is adamant that it is still not a restaurant.

She adds:

> In a restaurant you get waitress service and fancy carpets. And you can be served with salads and dessert and coffee. Here we don't do any of that. We're very basic, although I like to think that we're more homely, with a nice atmosphere. All I serve are cold sea food platters. I don't cook any fish at all. The only thing I cook is the mussels, and then only in the winter. That's why I can't call it a restaurant. I allow people to bring in their own bread and wine, but that's all.

It all sounded a little bit rustic and spartan, but there was definitely a unique appeal here, and I wondered how it had all developed into such a Mecca for connoisseurs. Heather explains:

> For the first two or three years we didn't do anything with it all, but then I did start to sell a few crabs and shrimps at the window. I was only doing it at weekends, but after a couple of summers my niece Kate left school and came to work for me on Saturdays. She wanted to work full time, so finally I did open it up to sell fish all through the week.
>
> We were just selling wet fish for people to take home, but there were a couple of old tables in here, and sometimes people would buy something like cockles or shrimps and just sit here and eat them. In those early days I was not even selling any oysters, although Richard's family has always been in the oyster fishing business. At that time he was in business delivering fish from Mersea to other markets, and he was supplying one customer with oysters just down the road, so it didn't seem diplomatic to go into direct competition.
>
> Anyway, we were getting busy here at the Shed, although I still wasn't working full time, or putting my heart and soul into it. Then Richard lost his wholesale business.

All his lorries went and all his drivers were made redundant. I even had to make Kate redundant. Virtually all that we had left was this old shed. So, at that stage, I had to start working myself and try to make a go of it.

Before long she was able to re-employ Kate and now she has a staff of four to help her run an enterprise that is often too hectic. There are days when Heather would prefer the pace to be just a little bit slower, so that she could have more time to enjoy it.

The seating arrangements, like the whole phenomenon, just grew gradually, without any design or formal planning. A customer offered her another unwanted table, and then another customer threw out some old church pews which also found their way into the Shed.

More and more of her customers took to sitting down to enjoy their cockles, prawns or oysters on the spot. Then some of her customers asked if they could bring in a bottle of wine. Heather agreed, and now a simple blackboard on the wall cordially invites customers to bring in their own bread and wine. The unique aspects of The Company Shed were taking shape, and its reputation for the excellence of its oysters and its huge sea food platters began to spread far and wide.

Now Richard is again concentrating on his wholesale oyster business, although he spends a lot of his time helping Heather with The Company Shed, which, like a runaway train seems to have built up a momentum all of its own. Publicity like the Rick Stein's food show has obviously helped, and at one stage it seemed that every few minutes a car would pull into the garage in the village to ask for directions to: 'That Shed place where they do all the great seafood.'

However, many of those initially just curious visitors do come back again and again, so it cannot be just the novelty and the publicity which has put West Mersea so firmly on the culinary map. Heather's seafood platters of fresh cockles, creek-fattened oysters, juicy red shrimps, succulent white lobster and crab, and a whole variety of smoked fish, are a gourmet's delight. So much so that there is now a second blackboard which quite often has a waiting list of people queuing up for tables.

Essex is the centre of the oyster cultivation industry in England, and my brief investigation has left me with the impression that it is in good hands. Richard, William and their colleagues have a careful eye to the future, not only re-laying to preserve their own stocks, but working hopefully to returning the whole river to plentiful production.

Eventually the Gigas oysters did thrive, so currently they are harvesting wild spawn Gigas oysters, dredging them up as before and re-laying them in the creeks.

The annual Colchester Oyster Feast looks set to continue indefinitely, so if you are one of the Mayor's invited guests, good luck to you. If not, you can always pop down to The Company Shed, where you will be served with a delicious plate of Essex oysters.

CHAPTER TWELVE

THE CHARM OF THE CHELMER

T he infant Chelmer starts in the heart of Uttlesford, the beautiful north-west corner of Essex, in a rich and rolling agricultural landscape with a wealth of small historic towns and picturesque country villages. Thatched and timber-framed cottages abound, white may blossom drowns the hedgerows in spring, and the corn fields are golden in summer. Birds whistle and warble in leafy lanes. The cool bends of the wandering stream harbour mallard and moorhen and the occasional swan. Get far enough away from the traffic-snarling horrors of the M11 and busy Stansted Airport, and this is a pastoral paradise.

Thaxted is the first town the river passes, perhaps the prize jewel in the Essex tourist crown, with a distinctly mediaeval flavour. The skyline in summer is unforgettable. The red-brick tower of John Webb's Windmill rises up from a field of golden rape with white sails spread out against a summer-blue sky. From the heart of the town beyond, the magnificent tower and spire of the Church of St John the Baptist soars 180ft high between puffball white clouds.

The windmill was built around 1804 and is fully restored. The church is much older, dating from between 1340 and 1510, and is almost a cathedral in size and splendour. It is faced in cobbled flint with a rich tracery of arched windows and two massive porches, one given by King Edward IV and the other by the Duke of Clarence. The king's porch shows the King's Arms, and the duke's is marked with his coronet.

However, both the windmill and the church are eclipsed by Thaxted's main attraction. A stone's throw from the church, down cobbled Stoney Lane with its mediaeval overhang of ancient shops, stands the lovely old grey and white, timbered guildhall. The ground floor is open, with two widening upper stories supported on massive wood posts, and for over 500 years it has dominated the heart of the town. The wool trade and the manufacture of cutlery made the town prosperous in the Middle Ages, and the guildhall was built by the Guild of Cutlers.

The guildhall has a number of long standing fifteenth-century neighbours, which do not really deserve to be pushed so firmly out of the limelight. There is also a lovely old row of early eighteenth-century almshouses on the approach to the field path to the windmill which should not be missed. Thaxted really does have an over abundance of ancient glories, but it is a lively and thriving little town.

It has an annual Spring Morris Weekend, when more than a score of visiting Morris sides can assemble to support the home team, the Thaxted Morris Men, in the renowned Morris Ring. It is a two-day celebration of dancing, leaping and stick-thwacking that ends with the haunting Abbots Bromley Horn Dance. The event is part of the parish church patronal festival, and is fixed on the Saturday evening nearest to 24 June ,which was the birthday of St John the Baptist.

The Thaxted Morris Men are resplendent in white trousers with pink candy striped waistcoats and flowery straw hats. They were formed in 1911, although there are records of the old forms of Molly dancing being performed in Thaxted long before then. The Morris Ring was inspired by the 'Travelling Morris', who toured the Cotswolds with tents and bicycles in the mid-1920s in order to revive the traditions of morris dancing in the villages. From this energetic beginning, a federation was established in 1934 with the aim of bringing morris sides into more contact with each other, and to encourage the formation of new sides. The inaugural meeting was held at Thaxted, where the vicar did not object to dancing on the Sabbath, and so the church link and a church service are a vital part of the proceedings.

In the seventy years between 1934 and 2004 there have been 276 Morris Ring meetings and Thaxted has hosted sixty-five of them. The morris dancers themselves have become a popular and familiar sight through summer evenings and weekends all over the country, performing regularly outside pubs, on village greens, and at any event that will have them.

Thaxted guildhall.

Later, in mid-Summer, comes the slightly less flamboyant but equally prestigious International Music Festival, following a tradition set by the composer Gustav Holst, a one time resident of Thaxted. Holst lived in Town Street. He was an organist at St John's Church and organised the town's Whitsun Music Festivals between 1916 and 1918, and somehow found the time here to write at least part of the *Planets Suite.*

Move a few gentle miles down the valley and the Chelmer passes through the tiny but charming villages of Great and Little Easton. There are old Roman tiles built into the walls of the church at Great Easton, and traces of an old Saxon fort mound in the grounds of Easton Hall. At nearby Tilty there was once a twelfth-century Norman abbey.

Great Dunmow, another ancient and attractive little town, comes next, and here the Chelmer becomes more of a river. The name means 'Hill Meadow', or perhaps 'Hill Fort', and the town lies on the route of the old Roman road from Colchester to St Albans. It became another thriving mediaeval town and when St Cedd brought Christianity to Essex in the seventh century, it was even larger and more prosperous than Chelmsford.

The focal point here is another splendid old building, the Old Town Hall, black-timbered, pastel blue and white plaster, with the upper storeys overhanging Tudor fashion, a high, sharp gable, and a small top tower. It is now converted inside to commercial use, but is still an immediate photographer's delight.

Other photogenic highlights include the Doctor's Pond, the Clock House, and the parish church. The pond is almost a small lake, a cottage and willow flanked haven of blue. The name is derived from a former town doctor who used the pond to breed and keep the leeches he used as part of the

Great Dunmow; Old Maltings.

medicine of his day. The smart black railings which prevent pedestrians from falling in from the path by the main road were erected to commemorate the Golden Jubilee of Her Majesty Queen Elizabeth II in 2002. Their design incorporates a golden crown and the town council shield, and they too can make a nice photographer's frame. The pond is also famous for the fact that Lionel Lukin's first unsinkable lifeboat was tested here.

The Clock House is gorgeous in red-brick, the high Dutch gables and the arched gateway practically radiant in full sunshine. It was built in 1586, and was the home of Anne Line until she was executed for the crime of sheltering Catholic priests. She was named a martyr and a saint.

There is also a beautifully restored timber-framed, red-tiled maltings with its conical kiln that has been dated back to 1565. Its beer brewing days are sadly over. It ceased operations in 1948, but it is a listed building with a new lease of life. It now houses a conference centre and a fascinating town museum.

In mid-summer, the town centre was hung with flags and bunting for the forthcoming Flitch Trials which are held every leap year. The origins of this mediaeval pageant go back to the priory which was once established at Little Dunmow, but the custom was happily revived in 1855. The prize is a flitch, or a side of bacon, and is awarded to the couple who can prove to a judge and jury that they have been happily married for a year and a day.

The charming old flint Church of St Mary the Virgin was built in the decorated and perpendicular style in the fourteenth century. It seemed the obvious place to keep the flitch chair, but it is actually kept at the church in Little Dunmow. However, St Mary's is still worth a visit.

The Chelmer winds on, past Felsted with another charming old guildhall

Felsted guildhall.

This charming old Tudor building in Great Waltham was probably a guildhall.

standing side-by-side with the church. The church was built in stages between the twelfth and fourteenth centuries and has a fine Norman tower. The guildhall dates back to the early 1500s when it was built for the Trinity Guild. It later became a school.

Further down the valley, lost in green country lanes, is the magnificent red-brick, towered Elizabethan manor house that is Leighs Priory. Close by, on a crossroads of the A131, is St Anne's Castle, a public house reputed to be the oldest in England and haunted for good measure. The river itself passes between the villages of Great and Little Waltham. The former has another splendid church with an ancient Tudor house with high-reaching chimneys by the end of the churchyard. The house is known as the guildhall. A description which suggests some uncertainty, but it certainly looks like a guildhall, and the location would be exactly right.

And so the river comes to Chelmsford, the County Town of Essex. In Roman times the settlement here was known as *Caesaromagous,* or Ceasar's Market Place. In the Middle Ages it grew to receive its first market charter in 1199, and became the County Town in 1218. The nineteenth century brought more trade and new industry, especially the radio industry, for it was here that Guglielmo Marconi developed the revolutionary new concept of radio, and established the first radio factory in the world.

Chelmsford's old Stone Bridge.

The first publicised entertainment broadcast in England was made from here in 1920, and two years later the new British Broadcasting Company was formed. The rest, as the cliché goes, is history.

The balustraded arch of the Stone Bridge in the centre of the town spans the River Can, which joins the Chelmer so that the town is flanked by rivers on two sides. From the bridge, the lively High Street leads up to the massive, square front of the Shire Hall, built in 1791. It has three entrance archways, topped by four Doric columns, above them a triangular gable and between them three plaques representing Wisdom, Justice and Mercy.

Behind the Shire Hall is Chelmsford Cathedral, a magnificent perpendicular Gothic church. As cathedrals go it is one of the smallest in England, yet it ministers to one of the largest diocese. The first church on the site was built in the eleventh century, and replaced in the fifteenth by the present building. The high nave ceiling is pale blue, patterned in white and gold, and together with high arched windows and a cream limestone floor creates a wonderfully light and spacious interior.

Where the rivers meet they flow past Moulsham Mill, a white-boarded landmark for more than 100 years. It was producing flour until 1963, but now it has been refurbished and houses a variety of artistic and creative crafts.

Chelmsford Cathedral.

The Chelmer flows on through woods and fields and the tranquil joys of the Essex countryside, until at last it joins with the Blackwater. We are now in the 14 miles of the old Chelmer and Blackwater Navigation, where in its nineteenth-century heyday a dozen locks helped to lift lighters and barges from Maldon to Chelmsford and to every waterside wharf in between. Many of the barges were horse-drawn, but at Heybridge Basin a sea lock enabled brigs and other small sailing craft to enter the new waterway. It was a vast improvement on the old pack mules and wagons, and the increased flows of timber, coal, corn and iron, all helped Chelmsford to thrive and grow.

Alas, the golden age of the old canals is over, it could only last until the coming of the railways, but this once thriving artery for trade has a new lease of life with the leisure industry. Cruising, canoeing, fishing, bird-watching or just walking the old towpaths are the new activities of today. At Heybridge Basin, the Old Ship Inn, which once served the navvies, seamen and bargemen of yesteryear, still serves fine food and ales to modern anglers and holiday-makers. It stands beside white weather-boarded cottages and overlooks the canal entrance and the small boats at the waterside, making another charming snapshot of traditional Essex.

All along its banks and throughout the valley the Chelmer has much to offer, in any season. Explore it as and when you can, and you will not be disappointed.

CHAPTER THIRTEEN

THE SONG OF THE CROUCH

The song of the Crouch is the cry of the gulls, the creak of a sail and the whisper of wind over water. It is the soft sound of the waves as they ripple against the river wall, the swift flap of goose wings as they soar overhead. It can be a wild roar of storm and rain, or a dancing interplay of sun beams and light. The river and the estuary, with its surrounding creeks and the incoming Roach, are a playground for sailors and seabirds, and the marshes are vital feeding and breeding grounds for great flocks of geese and waterfowl.

The Crouch begins in the small streams to the west of Wickford, which it circles under three bridges, but it is not until the tidal head at Battlesbridge that it begins to widen out into the salt waters of the estuary. Here is the last bridge across the river, and the highest reach for boats and barges. When the tide is out half a dozen small craft, all looking well worn or near derelict, lie hard against the mud, or pulled up on to the grass banks below the last of the old mills.

Towering six storeys high, the mill is a massive black-boarded structure on top of solid brick walls. It is the largest in Essex and now serves as an antiques centre with over eighty dealers displaying their wares on the first five of its rambling floors. The top floor is a long, narrow coffee shop where the high views through its small, lace-curtained windows look down on the moored boats and the river, not much more than a creek at low tide, meandering seaward through the green marshlands.

A few miles from Battlesbridge, on the north bank of the Crouch is the riverside town of South Woodham Ferrers, built in the 1960s. Here one of those typical white-boarded Essex clock towers rises above the Asda supermarket and a smart, modern, traffic-free town centre of red-tiled, red and yellow brick buildings. Between the town and the river, at Woodham Fen, you can find riverside trails with more views of the Crouch.

You can continue down the Crouch Valley by road, or you can let the train take the strain and use the Crouch Valley rail line. Either way, your next stop will be North

Boats at Battlesbridge, the tidal headwaters of the Crouch.

Fambridge, a peaceful little village dominated by the Fambridge Yacht Haven. On the west side of the village is the ultra-smart modern marina, with 180 berths at its long pontoons. It was formed in 1973 from Stow Creek, set between the salt marshes and farmlands. Viewed on a fine spring day, the sunlight sparkles everywhere, from the blue waters, the polished white hulls, the gleaming chrome and brass, and from scores of glittering silver mastheads.

Go back through the village and the road takes you down to the Yacht Centre. Just before you reach the river you will find the old white-boarded Ferry Boat Inn, dating back to the fifteenth century and said to be haunted by one of the old ferrymen. The last stretch of dirt road leads right to the water's edge, but don't park your car too close. It is a tidal river and the road floods. On your right now are the mudflats, with the marina beyond, and on your left the Yacht Centre boatyard.

The white-boarded Yacht Centre Club House juts out over the river, whilst beside it a small hammerhead landing stage reaches out to deeper water berths. There are boats moored out there. Looking inland across the flat marshes, past the boatyard, was Fambridge, and away to the right a patchwork of green fields with scattered flocks of sheep, all shrunk into lambs by the distance. In summer a field of yellow rape graces the far skyline.

From here you can walk along the top of the high earth bank that is the sea wall down to Althorne, about 5 miles away. The wall sweeps and curves initially in a series of loops, walking you above the level of the river and, on the inland side, the

The river wall at North Fambridge.

predominantly flat marshlands. On the river side, the wall is a long chequerboard slope of square concrete slabs. On the inland side a narrow creek runs parallel to the wall, where shelduck poke their vivid red beaks hungrily into the mud, like two sedate old ladies with coffee-coloured shawls over their white shoulders.

The land here is the Essex Wildlife Trust's, Blue House Farm Reserve. When last I visited rooks and magpies were fluttering in and out of the distant sheep, dots of black amongst the white like a slowly moving chess game on a green board. A grey heron sailed across the marshes on large flapping wings. Geese in pairs, and then a six-winged V formation flew overhead. There was a single white yacht sail moving along the river. The breeze was keen and refreshing and the clouds sailed high. It was all very calm and peaceful.

Once it was not so peaceful on the far side of the river. In 1016, Viking longships filled this broad stretch of the Crouch and at Ashingdon on the far side the Danish Army of King Cnut met the Saxon forces of Edmund Ironside in bloody battle. Edmund had twice beaten the Danish invaders, and confidently expected to win the third decisive battle that would expel them at last from England. But Edmund was betrayed by one of his key commanders. At the crucial moment, Eadric who led Edmund's Mercian allies, changed sides. The Saxon Chronicle says that he betrayed his lord and king, and all the people of English kin. The battle was lost, and almost all the leading Saxon Earls and leaders were killed in slaughter, although Edmund managed to escape with his life.

The marina, Burnham on Crouch.

Edmund swallowed the bitter pill and signed a peace treaty which made Cnut King of England for the next twenty-five years. Later Cnut, returned to Ashingdon to consecrate a Church in memory of the souls of the men who had been slain. Today the small church of St Andrew stands upon the same spot.

However, all this was almost a thousand years in the past. Today it is white yachts and not the square brown sails of Viking longships that rule the Crouch. Keep walking along the river wall and eventually you will come to Althorne and the yachts and cranes of Bridgemarsh Marina, which has more of the feel of a working boatyard. Here old boats and boathouses spill down the grass slope to the river. On the seaward skyline further down the river are the hazy outlines of more cranes and a first glimpse of Burnham.

Your car, or the blue, grey and silver train, will take you on to the old world charm of Burnham, the acclaimed 'Cowes of the East Coast', and the main yachting centre on the Crouch. It is said that very few people pass through Burnham, because there is very little beyond, and who would want to go further having discovered the wealth and attractions of its ancient maritime and sailing traditions? Hundreds of thousands of visiting day-trippers and small boat sailors obviously do not.

There is an elevated car park that overlooks the vast oblong basin of the yacht marina. There are moorings for 350 yachts here and a slight breeze rattling the dense forest of masts and stay wires will greet you as you walk past to find the broad sweep of the river. A small, railed observation point overlooks the marina opening, with the mass of

Above: At Burnham, ramshackle jetties stretch out into the river.

Right: Burnham on Crouch, the Jubilee Clock Tower.

Houseboats along the river at Burnham.

moored yachts on one side, now revealed in four neat lanes along the pontoons, and on the other the sun glistening on grey-brown mudflats that sweep out to the Crouch itself. The whole length of the river now a distant forest of more boats and mast heads, stretching inland and seaward as far as the eye can see.

You can walk towards Burnham, with the Riverside Park on one side and along the riverfront a row of picturesque old barges with houseboats built on top. Great links of weed-trailing mooring chains droop and loop across the mud. Beyond them, more ancient wooden jetties stretch out over the mud into the river and all are festooned with black weed. The Burnham Sailing Club and the Crouch Yacht Club are both smart-painted white clapboard buildings, where visiting yachtsmen are welcome.

Soon you will be walking along the red-brick paved promenade, where the river-front houses are all a mixture of red-brick and fresh white clapboard bays and balconies. The whole town and the old quayside has a fresh and breezy air, overlaid with a cocktail of scents with the definite tang of the river and the sea. There are rich colours too, and I had to stop and photograph the Cabin Dairy Tea Rooms, where the white column porch and the tiny garden were absolutely bursting and overflowing with packed flowers and flower-baskets.

There are two more yacht clubs, both patronised by members of the Royal Family. The Duke of Edinburgh is patron of the Royal Burnham Yacht Club. The Royal Corinthian, a white wedding cake building with blue-framed windows with a series of four tiers of railed balconies overlooking the river, is patronised by the Princess Royal.

Back from the waterfront, the town centre is dominated by a splendid octagonal clock tower, white-boarded above red-brick, which was raised in 1877. When it is not overcrowded, on carnival and regatta weekends, there is a gentle elegance in the main street with its Georgian shop fronts. Despite being a popular resort for visitors, there are no brash funfairs or amusement arcades. Burnham knows its place and its business, and its place is the riverside, and its main business is boat-building and boat servicing. In 1996 a new lifeboat station was completed, and volunteer crews maintain two inshore lifeboats.

For the land-lubber who has no boat of his own there is a ferry service over to Wallasea Island, where there is another large, purpose-built marina, or boat trips to view the wildlife and the red and golden sunsets along the river. The bird life here on display can range from wildfowl and waders, such as avocets, curlew and golden plover, to circling or hovering prey birds such as kestrel and harriers. Alternatively there are boat trips out to the seal colony near the river mouth. The latter trips are timed for low tide when the seals can be seen lying up on the exposed sandbanks. This is an especially delightful trip in early summer when the new pups are born.

However, the seemingly over abundance of yacht clubs seems to sum up Burnham, for the heart and soul of this little town is the world of yachting. It was the arrival of two London Yacht Clubs, the London Sailing Club and the Royal Corinthian, and their first informal races in 1893, which kick-started Burnham's growth into the premier yachting centre that it is today.

At any time the river will be filled with boats, but Burnham Week, always the week starting with the last bank holiday weekend of the year, is the highlight of the sailing calendar. It's a world-famous week of racing and regatta, when the flags and bunting will be flying, the river will be overflowing with the white and brightly coloured sails of the participating yachts, and the town with be bursting and buzzing with a multitude of visitors.

That buzz, with all the cries of the gulls, the creak of ropes and rigging and the flutter of a brisk sailing breeze, is all a part of that glorious song of the Crouch.

CHAPTER FOURTEEN

ESSEX CHURCHES

The lovely little Saxon church at Greensted near Chipping Ongar is said to be the oldest surviving wooden church in the world. The walls were built using upright split logs and the wooden tower is topped by one of those delightful spire belfries that are common in this quiet corner of south-west Essex. It is believed that there was a site of pagan worship here long before St Cedd arrived in 654 to inspire the building of this first Christian church.

When the Normans arrived there was another great surge of mediaeval church building. In addition to their passion for castles and great abbeys, the Norman knights also encouraged the addition of many solid square towers to enlarge the existing Saxon churches. However, the county landscape is also liberally sprinkled with round tower churches, and more of those eye-catching shingle spires.

Most of those churches have endured ever since, changing in shape or size as they have grown up with the towns and villages that embrace them. Today the church is still the heart of every Essex community, the focal point of every town and village, the essence of its heritage and history. Most of them have seen centuries of worship and prayer. They have witnessed, and still witness, all the rights of passage, through birth, marriage and death. They glorify the majesty of God. They are also splendid buildings in their own right, often masterpieces of mediaeval architecture, treasure troves of art and sculpture, in richly stained glass and lovingly carved wood and stone.

As the churches care for and nurture their communities, so the buildings need care and nurture in return. In Essex there are 600 Anglican churches, plus the Roman Catholic churches, the Free Churches and all the other Christian denominations, and they need a staggering £3 million annually just to keep the fabric of the buildings maintained. Their congregations alone often cannot raise enough to cover the cost of major structural repairs, and to help raise the shortfall the Friends of Essex Churches work tirelessly throughout the year.

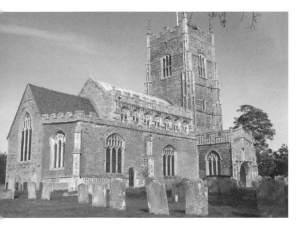

Clockwise from top left:

Cyclists assemble at the launch venue of the Church of St Mary the Virgin at Little Baddow.

The winning team for 2002 came from the Church of St Thomas the Apostle at Navestock.

Every boy's dream, young Jack Speakman poses with his cricketing hero Nasser Hussain.

The Church of St George in Great Bromley has received £12,500 for essential roof and masonry repairs.

One of their major fund-raising efforts is the annual sponsored Bike Ride & Walk, which takes place on the second Saturday in each September.

The idea is simple, to get as many people as possible to sponsor you, and then on the day visit as many churches as you can. Walking or cycling, it is a great healthy day out, spiritually and aesthetically rewarding, with the added plus of knowing that you have helped contribute to a very worthy cause.

In 2003, while I was researching this book, the event was publicised with a very well -organised launch day at the Church of St Mary The Virgin at Little Baddow, a lovely little square tower, flint church, which dates back to the Conquest. The England and Essex Cricketer Nasser Hussain came along to provide the essential celebrity interest, and to present the prize trophy of a small silver bicycle to the church group from St Thomas in Navestock, who had raised the record sum of £2,224, for the year 2002 event. The Ven. David Lowman, Archdeacon of Southend, blessed the whole enterprise in a short address.

In the photo-call that followed, Nasser posed with groups of participating cyclists, with the winning group from Navestock, and then signed autographs for eager fans. Young Jack Speakman, the grandson of Chairperson Anthea Speakman, also made himself the envy of all cricket-mad small boys by grabbing the opportunity to pose proudly with his hero.

To find out how it all went on the day of the Bike Ride & Walk, I later visited Marisa Petre, who had organised the launch, at the lovely sixteenth-century Ingatestone Hall, where she lives.

She answered cheerfully:

It all went very well. We had a perfect day for cycling and walking, and altogether we raised £122, 444. That's about £9,000 more than last year, and we are now supporting and involving the East London churches as well as Essex churches. Most counties in England have a similar Historic Churches trust, and thirty-one of them run sponsored Bike Ride & Walks on the same day, so it is a national event. This year we came third in the national table for funds raised, and that is very good. Our top fund-raising church in Essex for the 2003 event was Brentwood St Thomas, they raised £2,947.

The money raised is evenly divided. The person or church group raising the money can nominate which church they would like to receive half the amount, usually their own church. The other half goes into a central fund for general repairs. Any church in Essex and East London can apply for a grant from this central fund, and a grant committee processes applications and determines where the funds are most needed.

The Friends of Essex Churches was formed in 1951, and since 1984 the Bike Ride & Walk has raised almost £1.5 million. In 2002, eighteen churches benefited from grant funds, and this is about the average for each year. Every fifth year each church and chapel is inspected by architects, who report on the state of the building and the conservation work required. Problems such as damp and general decay, vandalism and atmospheric pollution, which is especially damaging to stonework, all mean that there is an on-going need to preserve and keep our churches for the benefit of present and future generations.

'We are very ecumenical in our outlook,' Marisa explained, 'and we support and try to involve all the Christian churches. Last year on the bike ride we had two Greek Orthodox Churches taking part, and the chapel at Tilbury Fort was also opened up for the day.' I asked if every church participates:

Every church makes an effort, but sometimes there are staffing problems. To have the church open means that someone has to volunteer to sit there all day between 10 a.m. and 6 p.m. We like to provide a welcome and refreshment like orange juice and biscuits, and of course, someone has to sign the sponsorship form. Some large churches will have a lot of people there, but at some of the smaller churches the whole day may fall upon just one or two pairs of shoulders.

The Bike Ride & Walk is the big fund-raising effort, but the work never actually stops and there are many other events throughout the year, and Marisa's list was impressive:

We have garden parties and concerts, coffee mornings and antiques workshops, a Christmas Fair, and we produce our own Christmas cards and postcards. We hold study days where a group will tour different churches to learn about their history and architecture. Our membership is around 650, and many people do work incredibly hard.

I noticed that last year one couple, Ray and Beryl Clements, had visited fifty different churches on their fifty-seven mile cycle ride from Chelmsford to Billericay. On the way they had also stopped off to sing at a wedding. I asked Marisa if this was a record, to which she replied:

Probably for 2003, but it's not the longest cycle ride we have ever had. In 2002 someone rode all the way from Ely Cathedral back to Shrub End, All Saints in Colchester which was sixty-four miles in six hours, although I don't know how many churches they actually managed to include along the way.

I left convinced that walking and cycling to visit churches is an ideal way to raise money for a worthy cause, but of course you don't have to wait until September and official sponsorship before you can make your visit. Due to the modern blight of deliberate vandalism, some churches are now closed when unattended, but most are open, and even when locked there is usually a note in the porch to direct you to the nearest keyholder. If you are not a walker or a cyclist you can always do it the lazy way and make your own tour by car.

You have all of Essex to choose from, and almost any church can be your starting point. However, Braintree District Council has produced a Time Trails Steeple Chase leaflet, as a guide to ten of the area's best.

Halstead, St Andrew's Church and the Jubilee fountain.

This particular trail starts at Rivenhall, a tiny village set just off the main road some three or four miles south-east of the town. Here, at St Mary and All Saints, is an east window containing the oldest stained glass in East Anglia, dating back to the twelfth century. The church trail swings north to Coggeshall and Holy Trinity with beautiful fourteenth-century wall paintings; still going north, the trail heads up to Halstead and the splendid St Andrews at the top of that steep High Street. Here the highlight is the canopied tomb of Robert, Lord Bouchier, who fought alongside the Black Prince at Crecy.

Next we come to St John the Baptist at Pebmarsh, and the oldest church brass in Essex, that of Sir William Fitzralph, set in a slab of purbeck marble. The route continues through by roads and charming countryside to St Barnabus at Alphamstone, famed for its picturesque setting at the far end of the village, and then loops east to St Mary's at Great Henny with its crooked spire.

Go due east now to Gestingthorpe and the Church of St Mary the Virgin. Here you will find a brass plate memorial to Captain Lawrence Oates, that 'very gallant gentleman', a member of Robert Scott's 1912 Antarctic Expedition, who deliberately walked out into a howling blizzard to die. Oates was suffering so badly from frostbite that he could hardly walk. He knew that he was slowing his comrades down and felt that his own sacrifice was necessary to enable his friends to reach safety. He disappeared from his tent with the immortal words, 'I am just going outside and may be some time.'

Still going east, another short country lane takes us to Little Yeldam, where the Church of St John the Baptist tops the hill. Here there is another link to one of the epic moments of our national history when the British flag dominated so many far-flung corners of the world. The year was 1900, the time of the Boxer Rebellion in China, and the man who led the British and Allied armies to lift the siege of the foreign embassies in Peking was General Sir Alfred Gaselee, the son of the rector of this church. The lectern here was donated by Sir Alfred in memory of his parents.

Next we come to Birdbrook and the picturesque Church of St Augustine, where, on a lighter note, a memorial plaque underneath the belfry commemorates Martha Blewitt who married nine husbands, although she only managed to outlive eight of them, and Robert Hogan who saw off seven wives. It seems a pity that they never actually managed to marry each other. Then the sparks might really have flown!

Finally the trail ends at Steeple Bumstead, and another church dedicated to St Mary the Virgin. Here there is a memorial plaque to Nurse Edith Cavell, the First World War heroine who was executed by a German firing squad for helping Allied soldiers to escape from Belgium. Before that she was the governess to the four children of the local vicar here. This brave young woman is also remembered in the church at Swardeston in Norfolk, coincidentally also dedicated to St Mary, where her father was the vicar.

At Steeple Bumstead the Steeple Chase trail ends, a main road leads straight back to Braintree. However, don't miss the chance to look at the old Moot Hall which stands

The old Moot Hall at Steeple Bumstead.

on the crossroads in the centre of the village. It is a lovely old timbered Tudor building with the usual overhanging upper storey. On the roof is a stone lion, holding up a shield which shows the Tudor coat of arms.

This one little loop through the heartland of Essex is an example of the delights that can wait on any short tour of Essex churches. Every spire and tower is a picture, usually in a delightful rural setting. Every nave and chancel is a cool haven of peace and prayer, every niche and corner revealing some hidden treasure, an ornate screen or tomb, a mediaeval font or lectern. Almost all of them have a story to tell, they are wonderful repositories of faith, heritage and history.

CHAPTER FIFTEEN

HERITAGE HIGHLIGHTS

From April to October is when the visitor attractions open up for the summer, all aiming to provide that perfect day out. The range of choice may be confusing, for Essex has an abundance of fascinating heritage sites and attractions. There are the castles and abbeys, farm parks and gardens, maritime jewels and idyllic villages that fill these pages, but this selection of five of the best will only attempt to look at some of the great land-owning halls and estates.

These places are not only an opportunity to look into someone else's big house, to view sumptuous rooms and furnishings and priceless collections of art and antiques, they are also steeped in the living history of both county and country. Essex is practically a rural suburb of London, and the great families who lived, and still live here, were often at the heart of affairs in the capital, close to their kings, and sometimes in the forefront of their battles.

A classic example is the lovely old high chimney, red-brick Tudor mansion of Ingatestone Hall, situated half way between Brentwood and Chelmsford, and once a manor of the ancient abbey at Barking. When Henry VIII demanded the Dissolution of the Monasteries, it fell to his Secretary of State, Thomas Cromwell, to carry out the task. One of Cromwell's most able assistants was a young lawyer named William Petre. It was Petre who visited Barking Abbey to draw up a list of its possessions and arrange their surrender to the king. He was in the perfect position to snap up the bargain of Ingatestone manor when it came up for sale.

Petre later became Sir William, Secretary of State to three successive monarchs, and as a valued elder statesman who was frequently consulted by the first Queen Elizabeth. Possibly to salve his conscience, he endowed an almshouse foundation for the poor, and then proceeded to build Ingatestone Hall in the form of a hollow square with a large central courtyard. The house has evolved and changed with time, but still stands in much the same form today. It is still the Petre family home.

The house is approached through a carriage-sized archway under a white-timbered Tudor gatehouse topped by a white clock tower, which bears the family motto in

Above: Ingatestone Hall, reflected in the placid waters of the lake.

Left: Ingatestone Hall, the clock tower.

the words *Sans Dieu Rien*, 'Nothing without God'. Once through you are into a vast courtyard. At one time there was an outer courtyard flanked by all the essential workshops and offices of a great estate, and then an inner courtyard through the west wing. Now a yew hedge replaces the old working buildings and the west wing is also long gone, leaving the one huge open space.

The house is now three sides of the inner courtyard, and the interior furnishings and decoration are all that you would expect of a stately home. The private family apartments are in the south wing, but the marvellous timber-panelled Stone Hall, the dining and drawing rooms and the Old Kitchen on the ground floor are all open to the public. There are some splendid walks around the gardens and grounds, and the best overall view of the house is from the far side of the lake.

Nearer to Chelmsford is Hylands House, an eye-catching, wide-winged, Grecian-style mansion that looks like a glorious white-columned wedding cake, with tall white chimney stacks instead of coloured candles. It is set in 570 acres of gently rolling and lightly wooded parkland. If it looks vaguely familiar then possibly you have seen it in a film or on a TV screen. It was once a stand-in for the White House in the Warner Brothers film *Chasing Liberty*.

Originally built around 1730, the house has seen several changes of ownership, and many enlargements and renovations. The house, park and gardens were all extensively remodelled when it was bought in 1789 by a wealthy Danish merchant who had

Hylands House, a magnificent white wedding cake, set in 570 acres of glorious parkland.

made his fortune in the West Indies. The landscape gardener and architect Humphrey Repton was approached for ideas and designs and was responsible for much of what we see today.

In the mid-1960s, after more changes of ownership, the house finally stood empty for a four-year period when it was further damaged by fire. It was then bought by Chelmsford Borough Council, which has set about its extensive restoration with the help of English Heritage. Nine spectacular rooms have been refurbished and the entrance hall has been restored to its full Georgian grandeur. The final stages of bringing it all back to its former glory were completed during 2005.

The gardens here are a maze of green lanes, opening out into lawns with circular flower beds, a stone-walled pond and a more natural looking pool. Since 1996 the extensive grounds have been the home of Chelmsford's annual music festival, the V Festival. In the north-east corner of the estate runs the gentle river Wid, and just across the river is St Mary's Church. In all it's the perfect event venue, or just come and walk, play and picnic.

Moving across the county toward Colchester, peacefully isolated behind a maze of small country roads and lanes, we find the soaring, breath-taking gateway tower of Layer Marney. Here we are back in the reign of Henry VIII, with the tallest and most elaborate Tudor gateway ever built in Britain. On a good, blue-sky summer's day, this glorious extravaganza of red-brick and terracotta embellishments can sparkle with an almost rosy brilliance in the sunshine.

It was built by Henry, the first Lord Marney, who was Captain of the Bodyguard to two English kings, Henry VII and Henry VIII. What we see, the north face, enormous though it is, is only a quarter of what was planned. Originally there was an open carriageway beneath the gatehouse, which was to open into an enclosed courtyard with a continuing building on three more sides. The east, west and south wings were never completed, although a conceptual model on the top floor of the gatehouse shows how it might have looked. You can see it on your way to the roof, where a narrow circular staircase to the top of one of the towers leads you to panoramic views of the surrounding countryside.

Nestling among the trees below you have a clear, bird's-eye view of the red roof and red-brick tower of St Mary's Church, which was built at the same time as the house. The tombs of the First Lord Marney and his son are inside. The church, the red-brick, red-tiled Long Gallery, which was once a stable block for up to thirty horses and their carriages, and the large black timber barn, which pre-dates the house, are all clustered close around the house itself, making a unified complex. The neat clipped hedges, lawns, flowerbeds, stone urns and statuary give it all a mellow, languid atmosphere.

Cressing Temple, half way between Chelmsford and Colchester, is not a stately home, but it was the centre of a vast mediaeval estate. It was given to the Knights Templar by Queen Matilda in 1137. These were turbulent times between the first and

Layer Marney Tower, the tallest
Tudor Gatehouse in Britain.

second crusades and the order of these military monks had been founded to protect
European pilgrims on their way to the Holy Land. They became wealthy and powerful
and Cressing was just one of some 7,000 manors which they held across Europe. The
estate was farmed and functioned for profit and the proceeds were channelled into
funding for their holy task.

They became too powerful and wealthy and when they were suppressed some 200
years later, the lands at Cressing passed to the order of the Knights of St John, the
Baptist of Jerusalem. The Knights of St John were a similar order to the Templars, but
they had refrained from dabbling in politics and banking, and so had not made life so
uncomfortable for the jealous kings of Europe or for the Pope. They lasted in turn at
Cressing for another 200 years.

In 1540 the estate passed to the Smith/Nevill family, briefly becoming the site of
a splendid stately home. A great house was built, but all that remains now is the late

Above: The vast wheat barn at Cressing Temple.

Right: The magnificent front view of Audley End.

sixteenth-century, brick-walled Tudor garden. The house itself has gone with time, and in its place there stands the lovely old white-walled farmhouse which we see today.

What also remains at Cressing are the two vast mediaeval barns which date back to the time of the Templars. The barley barn and the wheat barn are two gigantic, timbered cathedrals. The great doors are wide enough for the horse-drawn, harvest-laden wagons to be driven through, and standing inside one can only marvel at the soaring array of massive posts, rafters, cross-beams and tie-braces that make up the frameworks of these stupendous structures. The mediaeval carpenters were masters of their art, and the elaborate joints they chiselled and axed out of these huge timbers has to be seen to be believed.

Finally we come to what has to be the stately jewel of Essex, and one of the finest and largest Jacobean mansions in the land. I first saw it many years ago, with white-clad cricket teams playing on the green, their reflections and that of the vast east front shimmering in the waters of the river that widens into a small lake as it cuts the house off from what was the old A11. Behind it are elegant formal gardens and more extensive parklands, all designed by Capability Brown. Charles II described it as, 'Too big for a king, but might do for a Lord Treasurer.' It is, of course, Audley End.

Despite the later monarch's remarks, the house was, in fact, designed at the beginning of the seventeenth century to provide accommodation for visiting royalty. Unfortunately its builder, Sir Thomas Audley, the First Earl of Suffolk, fell almost immediately from royal favour and so it failed to impress and serve its immediate purpose. However, despite many changes of ownership, it has now come down to us as a virtual treasure trove, a magnificent symbol of our heritage, looked after, aptly enough, by English Heritage. To walk through its luxurious rooms and apartments, with their high gilded ceilings, flowing drapes and furnishings, is to walk through a combination of ultimate aristocratic indulgence and a series of 'Aladdin's Caves'.

When I last saw it there was a bonus in that the Battle of Naseby was being enacted in the grounds behind the house. This was the turning point in the English Civil War, when the King and his Cavaliers faced Cromwell and his Roundheads of the new Model Army. Audley End has no connection to the battle, it just happens to have the ideal amount of open space and background to play the effective host.

In bright afternoon sunshine, the opposing forces lined up. Canons boomed, muskets cracked, and smoke belched over the battlefield. The two armies met in a sea of bristling pikes under waving battle flags. The King's cavalry and Cromwell's cavalry charged and counter-charged in a thunder of racing hooves along the flanks.

All the places visited stage exciting programmes of special events throughout the summer, and this was a perfect example.

CHAPTER SIXTEEN

GOLDEN SAFFRON WALDEN

Saffron Walden has two golden claims to fame. It is one of the ancient market towns of Essex which prospered and grew rich on the thriving wool trade of the Middle Ages. Sheep were literally the golden fleece of East Anglia, and here, as in Suffolk and Norfolk, the expanding cloth industry capitalised on its close proximity to the vast continental market just across the North Sea. A long coastline with easy access to France, Holland and Belgium brought legitimate trade as well as the traditional opportunities for smuggling and fishing.

Many of the river valley villages and towns which we have already visited, Colchester, Braintree, Halstead and Coggeshall, all enjoyed the same boom. The rivers provided the fresh running water for cleaning and washing the wool, and for easy transport to the sea. This was a time when East Anglia was one of the richest areas in England, a time of pious church-building and the age of the Great Trade Guilds with their splendid guildhalls and Moot Halls, some of which we can still find at Thaxted, Finchingfield, Felsted and Steeple Bumford. The guildhall which once graced the market place in Saffron Walden was demolished in 1847 to make way for the new Corn Exchange.

Raising sheep, shearing, spinning and weaving were all busy occupations from the fourteenth century onwards. Many of them were practiced by solitary workers and their families in their own rows of cottages or back yards. The demand was for yards of woollen cloth in different colours, and here Saffron Walden found its name and its second golden claim to fame. Dyeworks were established around the ruins of the old castle bailey, and the main dye used was saffron yellow from the fields of yellow crocus which soon spread for miles around the town.

The crop was also grown as a medicine and as a flavouring; the saffron production and the textile industry continued side-by-side until the nineteenth century. Then industrialisation in the north of the country slowly killed off the East Anglian wool industry, and the imports of cheaper saffron from Spain and the Middle East, together with the development of new artificial dyes, caused the eventual disappearance of those gorgeous yellow crocus fields.

However, Saffron Walden today remains as one of the most charming mediaeval market towns in the county. Its heart is still the old Market Square, flanked on the south side by the Town Hall, an elegant black and white mock Tudor building with high red-brick chimneys, projected over solid brick archways. It looks like a mediaeval guildhall but it isn't; it was only built in its present form in 1879. The old Corn Exchange on the east side, which was built in the same period, has Doric columns either side of the arched entrance and is topped by a clock tower, all in white stone Italian style. It is now used as the town library.

An elaborate drinking fountain, built in 1861, is the centre piece of this small but busy square, surrounded on market-days by fruit and vegetables, flowers and clothing stalls. Here one thing has not changed, as shoppers browse for the best bargains.

From the Market Place head north and bear left and you will come to the old castle site, where the broken flint-rubble humps of the foundations of the old keep in a small grass park are all that remain of Geoffrey de Mandeville's once proud fortress. It was ordered to be made indefensible as a military stronghold by Henry II in the year 1158. Since then the trials of weather, the vandalism of looters and the passing of the centuries have all conspired to wear down the remains.

Wander west down Castle Street and you will pass a charming row of black and cream, black and red, purple, pink and blue cottages

The Town Hall. A glorious mock Tudor overhang can be seen over the stone archways.

The peaceful picture postcard village of Wendons Ambo.

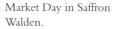

Market Day in Saffron Walden.

to remind you of how ancient this town is. At the bottom of Bridge Street there is another Tudor row in red, pink and white, with red tile roofs, a black and brown herring bone gable and pargeting panels of shells and squares. The nearby Eight Bells is a sixteenth-century inn, and the old black and white timbered building that is now used as a youth hostel dates back to the fifteenth century. In total the town claims some 400 buildings which are of special architectural and historic interest.

A short walk from Bridge Street will take you to The Common, which was formerly the old Castle Green. In the past this site has seen regular fairs, feasts and circuses, and once in 1252 a Royal Tournament, where one of the participating Norman knights was killed. In the eastern corner you will find the largest example of a spiral turf maze in the world, and one of only eight in England. The maze is believed to be at least 800 years old, and if you follow the spiral faithfully from the beginning to the centre you will have added another mile to your stroll around town.

There is a second maze in the Bridge End Gardens, this time a more conventional Victorian hedge maze. Nearby is the Anglo-American War Memorial, dedicated to all the USAF airmen of the 65th Wing Fighter Groups who lost their lives in the Second World War.

As you move back towards the town centre you will have circled around the magnificent, soaring spire of St Mary the Virgin, which dominates the town from almost every angle. Cut back along Church Street and you will find beneath it the largest parish church in Essex. A Saxon church probably stood on this hilltop site before it was replaced by a Norman church around 1250. The church has undergone many stages of re-building since. The Guild of Holy Trinity influenced much of its growth as the town grew with the fortunes in wool. By 1790 that golden age was waning and the church had fallen into disrepair. It then went through another major restoration carried out by Sir John Griffin. It was Griffin, the First Lord Braybrooke, who restored Audley End House.

The present spire soars up a magnificent 193ft into the sky, and together with the top part of the tower was added in 1832. Inside the church, slender pillars and arches lift the high nave ceiling up to an impressive 54ft, where the centre bosses are carved in eleven variations of the Tudor rose. Fittingly, in the roof and spandrels, there are also many representations of the Saffron crocus.

Right: The tower and spire of St Mary the Virgin, one of the largest parish churches in Essex.

Below: Castle Street is a charming row of pastel-coloured houses.

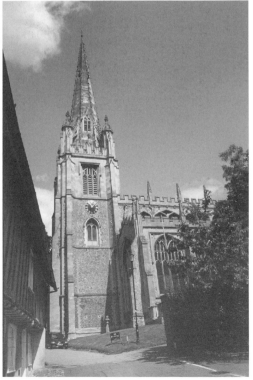

However, the jewel in Saffron Walden's crown, its most enduring and gorgeous attraction, has to be the Old Sun Inn. It occupies a corner midway between the Market Place and the church and is formed by a magnificent group of white washed, red-tiled buildings dating from the fourteenth century. Five lovely old gables overhang the street, all of them decorated with what has to be the most glorious display of pargeting in all of Essex.

This style of ornamental raised plasterwork was first used in Elizabethan times, and became very popular on half-timbered buildings in the seventeenth century. Here we have a riot of geometrical patterns, foliage and exotic birds, that date from 1676. Each projecting gable is a picture in its own right, but the most famous of all is above the square cartway that leads through to the rear courtyard. Here the hero of local legend Tom Hickathrift faces up to the Wisbech Giant over what appears to be a large wheel or the sun. Tom is armed with an axle for a club and a wheel for a shield, while the taller giant carries a staff or club.

The corner building is now a second-hand bookshop, with a helpful owner who can tell you what time of day you need to come back to find the afternoon sun highlighting the gables. A good browse will probably uncover a volume to tell you of the days when Oliver Cromwell stayed here and met with General Fairfax to plot their moves in the English Civil War.

The Old Sun Inn, with the most famous gable of them all featuring Tom Hickathrift fighting the Wisbech Giant.

Saffron Walden is the heart of the ancient district of Uttlesford, an area which also includes the other ancient market towns of Thaxted and Great Dunmow, which we have already visited. The great mansion of Audley End is almost next door, and the road past lovely little Wendons Ambo, with its picture postcard cottages flanking the close to the church, will take you down to Stansted Mountfitchet and its castle.

On the way you will pass through Newport, with its Elephant Green, named after a circus animal which dropped down and died there, and a Leper stone, where food was once left for the afflicted in the Middle Ages. You are almost within hearing distance of the traffic snarl on the modern M11, but in the heart of Newport you will find a sign detailing the fees for crossing the ancient toll bridge. It cost two pence for every wagon or cart and a penny for every horse or mule. Oxen, cattle and sheep were four pence a score. A single bull would cost you another four pence.

You are now close to all those charming little thatched and churched villages which we explored in chapter seven, which makes Saffron Walden the ideal centre for touring this part of Essex.

CHAPTER SEVENTEEN

ESSEX SHOWTIME

E ssex is not only a diverse and fascinating county, which makes it a joy to wander and explore. Essex also knows how to enjoy itself, and in the summer months from April through to September there is an almost endless parade of events and attractions. Much of it can be found in many other counties, such as the lavish agricultural shows, carnivals and festivals, open air concerts and open gardens.

The magnificent maritime events we have already mentioned, the Blackwater Barge Match, the racing and regatta weeks at Burnham and Brightlingsea. The annual Morris Ring at Thaxted attracts anything up to a score of morris sides and thousands of visitors, but morris dancing can be seen almost anywhere throughout the summer as the sides perform outside pubs and on village greens, and at almost any of the other events you can imagine.

In fact, morris dancing must be one of the oldest public dancing performances of all, and can be traced back 400 years to the time of the great Will Kemp. Will was a contemporary of Shakespeare, a dancing actor-cum-clown who was the original

Sailing up the Blackwater, the last leg of the Maldon Barge match.

Dogberry in *Much Ado about Nothing*. In the late sixteenth century he was part of the Earl of Leicester's Company which toured Holland and Denmark, and then for six years he was one of Chamberlain's Men, the acting company to which Shakespeare also belonged. However, his greatest claim to fame, the one honoured by Morris dancers everywhere, came at the turn of the century, when he danced all the way from the Globe Theatre in London to the city gates of Norwich, his celebrated *Nine Daies Wonder*.

To celebrate both the Millennium and the 400th anniversary of the original event, morris dancers all through East Anglia recreated Will Kemp's triumphant dance. Ten dancers covered the whole route, but at every stage the local morris sides were out dancing in relays, and practically every morris side in Essex took part.

Kemp told the story of his original dance in a small book which he published soon afterwards. Kemp danced through Whitechapel and left faire London. Clearly the urban sprawl of the capital was much less in those days. He continued on through Mile End and Stratford Bow, and by this time he claimed that there were thousands following him to watch his dancing. They urged him to drink, but knowing that he needed to stay sober if he was to last long enough to win his wager, Wise Will politely refused.

At Stratford Langton a bear-baiting had been prepared for his honour and entertainment, but such were the pressures of the multitude that he could only hear the bear roar and the dogs howling behind the crush, and so forward he went with his *hey de gais* to Ilford. From Ilford by moon-shine he danced to within a quarter of a mile to Romford, and there ended his first day's morris.

On the next day he returned to dance the last stretch into Romford, and then danced on merrily into Essex and Brentwood. It was market-day in the town and he reported that the multitudes were so great that he had great trouble in getting a passage through to the inn where he was to stay the night.

Even in those days large crowds attracted their fair share of ne'er-do-wells, and Kemp notes that during his visit to Brentford, two dy-doppers, or cut-purses were apprehended and brought to his inn, where he had to 'justly deny their acquaintance'. Fortunately he was believed. The criminals went to jail and danced upon the whipping cross before being sent back to London, but Will Kemp danced on through Essex. That same evening he tripped it on the next leg to Ingatestone.

His third day of dancing took him to Chelmsford, with never less than 200 in the crowds that followed throughout the day. Again it took him an hour to get through the town to his inn, where he locked himself in his chamber to rest. Instead he had to pacify the vast crowds with words from his window, for he was too weary to dance another step.

His next day's dancing, from Chelmsford on, he described as 'the heaviest way that any mad morris dancer ever trod'. It was a foul way through thick woods along lanes filled with mud-holes and great puddles. Two youths chose to dance along with him, hindering more than helping, until they came to a great splash of mud and water that filled the whole road. Kemp made a long leap that merely wetted his ankles at the far end, but one of the boys landed smack in the middle. Kemp laughed to see them 'labouring like two frogges', as one tried to help the other, and there he left them vowing they would never dance with him again.

In Braintree he was made warmly welcome, and he described the townsfolk there as an honest crew of kind men among whom he fared well, slept well, and was in every way well used.

Kemp spaced out his nine days of dancing with the permitted sixteen days of rest and danced on through Suffolk and Norfolk. On 8 March in 1600, he finally danced in through St Stephen's Gate into the city of Norwich. He had won his bet, although in some cases it proved not so easy to collect his winnings. Writing down his own tale was his way of countering the slanders of the London ballad-mongers who preferred their own versions, and of some of his reluctant creditors who maintained that his success was a lie.

Four hundred years later, the whole morris dancing world of East Anglia honoured their hero by dancing the same or at least a very similar route again. Will's story showed a fascinating picture of Essex in 1600, but modern traffic and modern changes meant that some diversions were now unavoidable. For the first few miles out from central London, the year 2000 dancers had to go by tube, but after that they kept as faithfully to the original route as was possible.

Today the spirit of Will Kemp's Nine Days of Dancing, and the Millennium Year re-creation, is still alive and well, as the Essex morris dancers continue their high-leaping traditions, in a jingle of bells, and a whirl of white handkerchiefs.

Thaxted Morris Men celebrating their big day.

Other echoes of Essex's past can be found at Hedingham castle, where each summer sees regular jousting tournaments and re-creations of mediaeval life. There will be displays of archery and falconry, strolling minstrels and dancing ladies, fanfares of trumpets, and of course the clash of swords and the thunder of charging horses.

The Knights of Royal England will provide heart-stopping action as they crouch behind their lances and urge their massive, gloriously canopied chargers down the jousting line. The crash of lance upon shield, the furious fights, the tumbling falls, are as authentic as you can get without anybody actually getting injured or killed. The flags fly and the crowds roar their applause, and the whole atmosphere is one of wild fun and heraldic splendour.

However, if all this noise and Middle Age excitement is too much, then for the re-creation of a more gentle period try the London to Southend Car Run. This annual classic car run organised by the South Eastern Vintage and Classic Vehicle Club is pure nostalgia. It is one of Southend's most popular annual events, and the original stimulus was to re-create the route that was taken by thousands of post-war Eastenders down the A13 to spend a day at the seaside.

When the cars arrive at Southend they flow in an endless stream of memories: the old Humbers, Fords, Wolseleys, Rileys, Hillmans, Triumphs, Jaguars and Rovers; everything from the zippy little open-top MG sports cars to the stately Rolls Royces and Bentleys. There are usually up to or over 300 classic and vintage cars on parade, all of them lovingly restored and polished, and gleaming like mobile mechanical jewels in the Southend sunshine.

Crossing the finish line at the Southend Classic Car Show

When I saw the show there was a Morris Minor, like the one my Aunt Mary used to own, the very first car in which I proudly rode as a back-seat passenger. An Austin A30, which was the first car that I actually owned, and a Ford Cortina, just like the one I used to pack all the kids in to take the family on those first holidays to Devon and Cornwall. There were so many memories for me and obviously just as many reminders for all of the thousands of visitors who had come to watch the annual London to Southend Classic Car Rally.

The broad sweep of the Esplanade, between the green cliffs and flower gardens on the one side, and the sea on the other, was the perfect place to park this magnificent slice of social and motoring history, with plenty of room for visitors to circulate and admire. Even those too young to have fond memories of a more leisurely bygone age, when motoring was actually a pleasure, could not fail to be impressed. These were not just antiques on display, they were cherished old friends, each one polished to perfection.

Most of them had started the run from the large car park at Billingsgate Fish Market in the Docklands at around 9.30 a.m. Others had started from the White Webbs Museum in Enfield. This was not a race, there was no rush or hurry, there was even a half way stop at the Ford Research Establishment at Dunton, where the cars had performed a leisurely lap of honour around the establishment's test track.

Finally, at about 12 p.m., they started rolling majestically into Southend. In ones, twos, and little streams they passed under the bold white banner with its WELCOME TO SOUTHEND ON SEA in large black letters. Loud cheers and applause greeted every new arrival, plus some jaunty 1930s' music from the yellow-shirted jazz band.

There were a host of pseudo celebrities on parade. Charlie Chaplain was helping to raffle a vintage car for charity, and so I was not surprised a little later to see Elvis directing traffic. At the far end of the Esplanade, where the double lines of parked vehicles were lengthening, I also found a contingent from *Dad's Army*. Captain Mannering was standing proudly by a 1939 white Riley 1214 Saloon, resplendent in full khaki uniform with binoculars and swagger stick, with Private Walker lurking in the background. Both of them were enjoying their roles. The Arthur Lowe look-a-like consented to pose for a photograph, but only after I had squared my shoulders, sucked in my belly and puffed out my chest in the approved military fashion. As he turned away I'm sure I heard him mutter, 'Stupid Boy', and Walker took the surreptitious opportunity to try and sell me a pair of black market nylons.

With the first few cars, the Pearly Kings and Queens arrived. They were Chris and Joan Friend, the Pearly King and Queen from the Isle of Dogs, Poplar, and Danny and Jackie Murphy, the Pearly King and Queen of Homerton Hackney, and the Princess Phyllis. The Pearly Kings and Queens have been around for 125 years, they told me, one pearly couple for every one of the old metropolitan boroughs, and two for the inner city, forty-eight pairs in all.

The Pearly Kings
and Queens, lending
their support to the
Southend Classic Car
Rally.

The Pearly Kings and Queens of London are the second oldest charity association in England. The titles are handed down through the families, as are the thousands of pearl buttons that are sewn in gorgeous and elaborate designs on their clothes. The clothes, of course, usually change with the wearers, although Danny's suit was sixty years old, having been previously worn by his Uncle Fred, a former Pearly King of Westminster, who was conveniently the same height and size.

Their founder was Henry Croft, an orphan boy who was born in 1862 and brought up in a Dr Barnardo's home. He had to leave the orphanage and start earning his own living at the age of twelve, and so he became a road-sweeper and rat-catcher in Somers Town market, which is near Kings Cross.

Young Henry soon noticed two things. One was that whenever the rich people walked down the street, or went rolling by in their carriages, then all the poor people would stop and gawp at all their fine clothes and rich jewels. The other thing was that in amongst all the rubbish he was sweeping up there were hundreds of saltwater mother of pearl buttons. Pearl buttons were cheap and common in those days, but when the light caught them they reflected a whole spectrum of colours, exactly like the bright flashes of colour that the rich had in their expensive jewellery. Henry collected up all the buttons he could find and sewed them in straight lines all the way up his trousers and waistcoat and all around his cap. He was the first Pearly.

In those days, before the National Health Service came into being, all the large London hospitals helped to support themselves with collection days. On one such day, Henry strolled up, all dressed in his suit of buttons, so they gave him a collecting bucket. Henry soon collected more pennies and ha'pennies than anybody else, so the next time they held a collection they asked him to help again.

The Pearly Kings and Queens grew out of that, because Henry soon found that he just couldn't cope single-handed with all the requests he was getting from the hospitals and churches, and any other organisation that was trying to raise money to help the poor, or the deaf, or the blind. In a flash of inspiration he hit upon the idea of the Pearly Families. He realised that if he could find one family in each of the London boroughs who would dress up and wear the buttons, then they could collect for their own local hospitals and charities.

Henry knew the markets and he knew the costermongers, he knew that these were the sort of people who could do the job and who would be willing to do the job. So he toured all the other markets in London until he found a family in each borough which was willing to be a Pearly Family. Then it became a tradition that all the families in buttons would turn up for the Bank Holiday Fair on Hampstead Heath, and then they started going to the Derby. Finally they were doing so much good charity work that Henry actually approached royalty and asked for permission for these families to use the titles of Pearly Kings and Queens, and for their children to use the titles of Pearly Prince and Princess – and he was given that permission. Then they all started to sew their titles on their backs.

Henry Croft finally died in 1930, and by then there were around 400 Pearly Kings and Queens and their families who attended his funeral, all in their pearly suits and hats and dresses. However, the fine tradition he started still goes on, with the Pearly Families still supporting charities and good causes throughout London and the surrounding counties. The whole purpose of the London to Southend Classic Car Rally is to raise money for charity, so it was almost inevitable that at least one Pearly King and Queen would be there in support.

In fact it is amazing the lengths to which some people will go to raise money for charity. Around Christmas there is the annual Maldon Mud Race in which hundreds of noble, or lunatic, souls race madly to and fro across the River Blackwater. The actual race day varies each year, depending on tidal conditions. The contestants have to race across the river, along the far bank and back again, slipping, splashing and sliding through the mud. Some of them briefly disappear, although the stewards usually manage to get them all out, eventually.

Another unique event was the Great Samba Ramble. When I saw it, Colchester's magnificent two-day festival was opened in grand style by the Mayor, flanked on either side by the mediaeval splendour of the Town Watch. Sunlight sparkled off the Mayor's chain of office, and from the silver helmets, breastplates, and bright steel pike blades of his formidable escort. It was a nice show of pageantry to start off the day, and from there on the fun and the spectacle never stopped.

There was street entertainment to suit all tastes, with clowns, cavemen, stilt walkers and a Chinese Dragon Dancer, all circulating through the crowds. The Swervy World Jazz Band were stomping and swinging in the doorway to Boots. There was a fire-eater breathing red flames while balancing on a one-wheeled bike in Lion Walk Square. The ladies morris side, Annie's Fantasies, were leaping high in the shade of the castle walls,

The then Mayor and Mayoress of Colchester, Nigel and Mary Chapman, performing the opening ceremony for the 2002 Festival with the support of the Colchester Town Watch.

Dancing through the heart of Colchester.

while the Arabian Belly Dancers were sinuously rotating their navels. There was music, comedy and street art, literally something for everyone.

The finale of that first day was the Great Samba Ramble, combined with a parade of splendidly fearsome Boudiccas in their hand-drawn chariots. It was Mardi-Gras in Rio, transplanted Colchester style and spiced up with a twist of British history and humour. They came down the High Street, past the Town Hall where the Mayor and the Town Watch were again lined up in a guard of honour. The bands played, the dancers danced, arms waved, skirts swirled, and everyone rocked and rolled. The long serpentine procession wriggled and writhed its happy musical march through the heart of Colchester, circling round to an exuberant finish at Lion Walk. It was vibrant, noisy, colourful and frenzied, and I'll swear they couldn't have done it better in Jamaica or New Orleans.

For Sunday the mood was more traditional, with a historic re-staging of the Great Cloth Fair, once an annual event in Colchester which originated during the reign of Edward II. Again there was an official opening ceremony, performed by the Mayor with the stalwart backing of the Town Watch. This involved the cutting of the Colchester Russett, a bolt of cloth for which Colchester became famous during the Middle Ages, when the merchants of East Anglia grew rich on sheep and the wool trade.

The rest of the day followed the theme of fleece into cloth, with demonstrations of carding, spinning, weaving and dying, leading up to the production of another finished bolt of cloth by the late afternoon. This was then inspected in the traditional manner, and fixed with the official lead seals of the town to certify its good quality.

Just about anything you can imagine that was linked with the wool trade was also being demonstrated or was on display. To make up all the fun of the fair there were more historical re-enactments, archery and tug-of-war competitions, ferret racing, and again a whole host of entertainers, dancers and musicians. Sadly the Great Samba Ramble came to an end as an annual event because public insurance costs soared too high, but it was a splendid example of what Essex can achieve.

Wherever you go in Essex, there will always be something special to see or do and a visit or telephone call to any of the county Tourist Information Offices will get you all the latest event updates on any part of the county.

Appendix

The numbers and office addresses for visitor centres featured in the book are listed below:

Southend on Sea Visitor Information Centre
Southend Pier
Western Esplanade
Telephone: 01702 215120
www.visitsouthend.co.uk

Chelmsford Visitor Information Centre
Chelmsford bus station
Duke Street
Telephone: 01245 283400
www.chelmsford.gov.uk

Colchester Visitor Information Centre
1 Queen Street
Colchester
Telephone: 01206 282920
www.visitColchester.com

Saffron Walden Visitor Information Centre
1 Market Place
Saffron Walden
Telephone: 01799 524002
www.visitsaffronwalden.gov.uk

Clacton On Sea Tourist Information Centre
Town Hall
Station Road
Clacton
Telephone: 01255 686633
www.essex-sunshine-coast.org.uk

Burnham-on-Crouch Community & Tourist
Information Centre
1 High Road
Burnham on Crouch
Telephone: 01621 784962
www.burnham.org.uk

Maldon Tourist Information Centre
Wenlock Way
High Street
Maldon
Telephone: 01621 856503
www.visitmaldondistrict.co.uk

Other titles published by The History Press

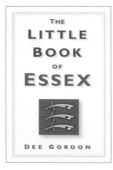

The Little Book of Essex

DEE GORDON

The little book of essex is packed full of entertaining bite-sized pieces of historic and contemporary trivia that come together to make essential reading for visitors and locals alike. It can be described as a compendium of frivolity, a reference book of little-known facts, or a wacky guide to one of england's most colourful counties. Dip in randomly, or read consecutively, there are no rules. Be amused and amazed at the stories and history of essex's landscape, towns, villages, heritage, buildings and, above all, its people.

978 0 7524 5127 2

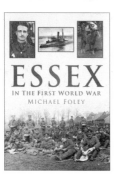

Haunted Essex

CARMEL KING

From heart-stopping accounts of apparitions, manifestations and related supernatural phenomena, to first-hand encounters with phantoms and spirits, this collection of stories contains both new and well-known spooky tales from around the county of Essex. Drawing on historical and contemporary sources, Haunted Essex contains a chilling range of ghostly phenomena. This phenomenal gathering of ghostly goings-on is bound to captivate anyone interested in the supernatural history of the area.

978 0 7524 5126 8

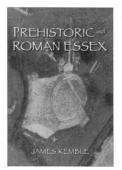

Essex in the First World War

MICHAEL FOLEY

Essex was a key area during the war. Situated on the east coast Essex was subjected to great danger and harsh times by the enemy in the form of air raids from Zeppelins, and later, from the more potent aeroplane attacks. This well-illustrated and informative book sets out the experiences of the county and its inhabitants against what was happening in the broader theatre of war. It offers a valuable insight into life for Essex folk in the First World War and will appeal to anyone interested in the county's history.

978 0 7524 5178 7

Prehistoric and Roman Essex

JAMES KEMBLE

Even those who live in Essex may be surprised by the richness of the county's prehistoric and Roman heritage, and the number of visible ancient monuments that can be readily seen, as detailed in this book. With its county maps, photographs and detailed gazetteer of the sites and monuments, this book provides the visitor and historian with an accessible guide from which to conduct their own exploration of Essex.

978 0 7524 5032 2

Visit our website and discover thousands of other History Press books.

www.thehistorypress.co.uk